**T**

David Ephraim Hart-Davies

BEHOLD THEREFORE THE GOODNESS
AND SEVERITY OF GOD
Romans 11:22

# THE SEVERITY OF GOD

## A STUDY OF JUDGEMENT HUMAN AND DIVINE

by

## D E HART-DAVIES, MA, DD

(Sometime scholar of Corpus Christi College, Cambridge. Author of *The Genesis of Genesis; Jonah: Prophet and Patriot* etc.)

2003

Quinta Press

Weston Rhyn

# QUINTA PRESS

Meadow View, Weston Rhyn, Oswestry, Shropshire, England, SY10 7RN

Visit our web-site: http://www.quintapress.com

Distributors in North America: Quinta Press,
19 Bridge Street, Millers Falls, Massachusetts, USA, 01349

*The Severity of God*
*First published* . 1943 by Pickering and Inglis Ltd, London
*Revised edition* . 2003

ISBN 1 897856 18 0

Printed by Quinta Business Services and bound by Principal Bookbinders,
Ystradgynlais, Swansea

# Publisher's Foreword

Readers may find some of the language in this book a little quaint and the illustrations slightly dated. This should not be wondered at since the book was first published in 1943 and the author died in 1946. But this should not put off a careful reading of this book. The last 150 years have seen continuous attacks on the credibility of the Bible as a true revelation of God's character and his ways of dealing with men. During the first half of the 20th century there were few men who were able and prepared to enter the battle against the Bible's detractors. As a result a false view of the Bible (a book full of untrue myths) and of God (only love who would never punish anyone) has been handed down to the present generation and accepted as true. Hart-Davies, in *The Severity of God,* seeks to uphold the Bible's view of itself as the infallible revelation of God which reveals God as a God of righteousness and justice as well as of love.

I would like to thank the author's family for granting permission to reprint this book, especially Mrs Jane Hogbin, one of the author's grand-daughters, who, with her cousin, provided the brief biography of the author. Thanks are also due to Dr Marianne James for proof-reading.

**Dr Digby L. James,** Quinta Press

# DAVID EPHRAIM
# HART-DAVIES

David Davies was born in Liverpool 25th September 1870, the second of six children (Winifred, David, Bessie, Sarah Anne, Hannah and Alice). His father was a foreman at the Liverpool docks and he died in an accident at the docks.

David went to Liverpool Grammar School. On leaving school he worked in an office (possibly construction) until he was 29. During this time he saved enough money to pay his own way through Corpus Christi College, Cambridge. He was subsequently ordained and became a curate at St Paul's and St Silas's Church in Blackburn. While there he was befriended by Thomas Hart, a local businessman and J.P., to whom the book *Jonah: Prophet and Patriot* (also published by Quinta Press) was dedicated.

In 1904 he married Thomas Hart's daughter Winifred and took her surname, thus becoming Hart-Davies. They had three daughters and two sons, one of whom died in infancy. His first living was as vicar at St James's, Carlisle and later moved to St Albans, St John's Wood and Christ Church Sidcup. His last post was as vicar of St Thomas's

Church in Edinburgh where he was involved with building a new church in Corstorphine Road.

During his ministry he undertook five day missions for the Bible Testimony Fellowship  and also Biblical lecture tours in Canada, the U.S.A., Australia, and New Zealand.

He wrote several short books defending the Bible from modern attacks, of which *Jonah: Patriot and Prophet* and *The Severity of God* are published by Quinta Press.

He died in 1946 on a Manchester railway station returning from a mission at which he had been the speaker.

TO MY WIFE
CONSTANT HELPMEET, DEVOTED MOTHER
A COMFORTER TO MANY
THIS BOOK IS GRATEFULLY DEDICATED

# PREFACE

DURING the past ten years I have been privileged to lecture on Bible subjects in various centres in the United Kingdom, and also in Canada, USA, Australia and New Zealand. Frequently I have been asked to publish several of the lectures delivered. In response, two of them are incorporated in this volume. But my principal aim has been to contribute something towards restoration of confidence in the Bible as the inspired Word of God. This is admittedly an indispensable condition of a new and better order after the war.

The appalling devastation of life and property with the unparalleled misery entailed in European lands and elsewhere has its main source in an apostasy which is rooted in unbelief in the Biblical revelation, especially in that of the Old Testament. But it is now becoming evident that the judgements of God in the present may be interpreted, at least in part, in the light of the judgements of God in the past. Some of these have been severely criticised and condemned. The authority of the Old Testament especially has been weakened thereby. It is my conviction, however, that a vast amount of prejudice exists through lack of knowledge of what the Bible precisely contains and reveals. To dissipate that prejudice forms a major part of my endeavour.

To attempt 'to vindicate Eternal Providence and justify the ways of God to men' is no easy task. It is much easier to criticise than to construct. God only can produce the exquisite texture and colour of a rose; any wanton child can pick it to pieces. This is especially true with reference to the Biblical records of divine judgement. Certain of these are here examined in detail. In doing this I have aimed to demonstrate that the goodness of God is not obscured but more clearly revealed through the apparent severity of his judgements.

I am indebted to certain friends, and not least to my wife, for many helpful suggestions. I have also to thank my kind neighbour, the Rev. Innes Logan, M.A., for the care which he has taken in the correction of the proofs.

**D.E. HART-DAVIES**
EDINBURGH

# CONTENTS

# Chapter 1

# Universal Depravity and the Deluge: But Noah

Now it came to pass, when men began to multiply on the face of the earth, and daughters were born to them, that the sons of God saw the daughters of men, that they were beautiful; and they took wives for themselves of all whom they chose. And the Lord said, 'My Spirit shall not strive with man forever, for he is indeed flesh; yet his days shall be one hundred and twenty years.' There were giants on the earth in those days, and also afterward, when the sons of God came in to the daughters of men and they bore children to them. Those were the mighty men who were of old, men of renown. Then the Lord saw that the wickedness of man was great in the earth, and that every intent of the thoughts of his heart was only evil continually. And the Lord was sorry that he had made man on the earth, and he was grieved in his heart. So the Lord said, 'I will destroy man whom I have created from the face of the earth, both man and beast, creeping thing and birds of the air, for I

am sorry that I have made them.' But Noah found grace
in the eyes of the Lord . (Genesis 6:1–8).

IN the Biblical history of mankind the judgements of
God occupy a conspicuous place. The life of man in
general has been so far removed from the ideal of his
Creator that a chastening process has of necessity been
in operation from age to age. It is patent that the true
relation of man to his Maker is broken. Moral disharmony
has resulted, due in the main to the persistent crime
which says, There is a God, but I prefer to act as though
there were none.

The Bible, however, to be precise, is not a history of
mankind; it is pre-eminently a record of redemption. It
is the sublime story, unparalleled in all the literature of
the world, of how the Almighty God whose throne is
established in righteousness, has dealt in the past with
that corruption which makes so foul a stain upon the
purity of his universe, and how he intends to deal with
it in the final consummation of the ages.

In the prophetic language of Isaiah, it is written, 'With
my soul I have desired you in the night, yes, by my spirit
within me I will seek you early; for when your judgements
are in the earth, the inhabitants of the world will learn
righteousness' (Isaiah 26:9). The question follows, What
can we in these critical days learn from the judgements
of God in the past? That represents my present endeavour.
This book is from first to last an Exposition—an attempt
not to present new truths, but to exhibit old facts concerning
the ways of God with men in a clearer light, with whatever
aid science and recent additions to our knowledge of
history can supply.

I have thought it desirable not to discuss the judgements of God in a general way, but to examine certain selected examples of divine action in the past in order to glean therefrom abiding principles for perpetual remembrance. For these things 'are written for our admonition, upon whom the ends of the world are come'.

At the outset, however, I am conscious of a tremendous obstacle in my path. We live in an atmosphere of incipient infidelity. Today the Bible records are too often obscured or ignored or derided, amid the welter of the transitory opinions of men. Especially in regard to the Old Testament is modern infidelity or practical unbelief most pronounced; and it is just there that the judgements of God are most vividly presented. But in our extremity God himself has intervened. While professors and preachers have been dumb, stones have been crying out, giving their own testimony to the dependability of that written Word of God which lives and abides for ever.

A revolution in the realm of Biblical scholarship has proceeded slowly but very surely during the past half century. Critical positions once thought to be unassailable are now freely surrendered by many who were once their foremost defenders. This revolution has been accomplished by means of the new facts of history which have been brought to light through the agency of the various archæological expeditions that have been at work in the Near East. What has ensued might be described as a battle of Bricks versus Cobwebs. The cobwebs may be said to symbolise those theories, conjectures and presuppositions of the Higher Criticism, which have been, dare we say, spun out of the imagination of speculative Continental professors and theologians, and too readily adopted by preachers and teachers in our own country. The Bricks, on the other hand, may be said to symbolise the tablets, bricks and monuments which have been unearthed in Egypt and Palestine, in Asia Minor, Persia and Mesopotamia, providing new facts of ancient history of an extremely illuminating character. The final result of the battle is not in doubt. In the words of the late Professor Sayce, 'subjective fantasies must make way for the solid facts of science which were at last being recovered. ... With hardly an exception the archæological discoveries of the last thirty-five years in the Nearer East have been dead against the conclusions of the self-appointed critic and on the side of ancient tradition.'

The testimony of Sayce here quoted has been immeasurably strengthened by the amazing discoveries of the two decades which followed the termination of the last war, issuing as it did in the opening up of territory in the Near East which had formerly been forbidden to the archæologist. The result is that the historic integrity of the Scriptures, both of the Old Testament and the New, has been vindicated to a degree which would have been deemed impossible at the beginning of the century. Yet old prejudices die slowly; and the need for the dissemination of the new knowledge is most urgent, as the following true story will illustrate.

Towards the close of the year 1928 there appeared in *The Morning Post* newspaper a report with the startling caption, printed in big bold characters: 'A Dean who does not believe in the Flood'! A meeting of the supporters of the Bible Society, drawn from the various Christian churches and denominations of a Midland town, had been held on the previous evening. A peer of the realm presided. The principal speaker was the Dean of a neighbouring cathedral. In the course of his remarks the Dean was reported in the press to have said: 'I do not believe in the Flood. I never did, and I was never asked to. I had a Noah's Ark as a small boy, and I may have treated it as an idol, but I never believed in Mr Noah'! Before the end of the meeting the noble chairman expressed his astonishment at the bold, not to say rash, statement of the Dean, and then gave his own testimony to the historicity of the Biblical record by adding: 'I myself have always believed in Mr Noah and in Mrs Noah also.'

Now within six months of the appearance of that report in the public press I was present at a meeting of students and others interested in archæology, in the lecture room of the University College, in Gower Street, London. Mr C Leonard Woolley, who has since been knighted, was presenting an account of the results of his exploratory work during the preceding season in the neighbourhood of the ancient city of Ur of the Chaldees, situated in southern Babylonia. At the end of his lecture he thrilled his audience by saying: 'We have proved the historical basis of the story of the Flood.'

## (1) THE EVIDENCE OF ITS HISTORICITY

Mr Woolley, who had been appointed, about seven years previously, the Director of the joint expedition of the British Museum and the University of Pennsylvania, has published a detailed account of his digging operations in Ur of the Chaldees and its vicinity in the season of 1928–29, during which quite unexpectedly he discovered evidence of a gigantic catastrophe similar to that of the Noachian flood. After digging down and down until they reached what appeared to be the bottom of everything, they were somehow encouraged to proceed further, when they made a phenomenal discovery.

The following is a brief extract from his own narrative.

The shafts went deeper, and suddenly the character of the soil changed. Instead of the stratified pottery and rubbish, we were in perfectly clean clay, uniform throughout, the texture of which showed that it had been laid there by water. ... The clean clay continued without change until it had attained a thickness of a little over eight feet. Then, as suddenly as it had begun, it stopped, and we were once more in layers of rubbish full of stone implements, flint cores from which the implements had been flaked off, and pottery. ... The great bed of clay marked, if it did not cause, a break in the continuity of history; above it we had the pure Sumerian civilisation slowly developing on its own lines; below it there was a mixed culture of which one element was Sumerian and the other of that al'Ubaid type which seems to have nothing to do with the Sumerians, but to belong to the race which inhabited the river-valley before the Sumerians came into it ...

Inundations are of normal occurrence in Lower Mesopotamia, but no ordinary rising of the rivers would leave behind it anything approaching the bulk of this clay bank; eight feet of sediment imply a very great depth of water, and the flood which deposited it must have been of a magnitude unparalleled in local history. ... Taking into consideration all the facts, there could be no doubt that the flood of which we had thus found the only possible evidence was the Flood of Sumerian history and legend, the Flood on which is based the story of Noah.[1]

In an article which appeared in *The Times* newspaper of 16th March 1929, entitled 'The Flood: New Evidence from Ur', Mr Woolley gives some interesting detail.

---

[1]  *Ur of the Chaldees*, pp. 26–29.

> Deeper we went and found more pottery, some of it of the types common in the earliest graves, but with this further examples of painted vessels and sherds of a sort hitherto unknown at Ur, and, at the very bottom, a burnt brick also of a type wholly new to us; this last proves that at the time when the painted pottery and the flints were in use, Ur was not merely a village of mud huts, but already a town civilised and properly built.

He concluded his article with the following weighty affirmation:

> He would have been an optimist indeed who had hoped to produce material evidence for such an event as the Flood of Sumerian legend, which is also the Flood of the Book of Genesis; but in no other way can I interpret the facts which our excavations here give us.

But this striking piece of evidence from recent archæological discovery does not stand alone. An alluvial deposit of wide extent was found at Kish, close to the site of ancient Babylon, about two hundred miles from Ur of the Chaldees. A report of the discovery appeared in *The Times* of 18 March 1929, from the pen of Dr Stephen Langdon, Professor of Assyriology at Oxford, and Director of the Oxford Field Museum Expedition to Kish. Two precipitations of clay, potsherds, and stranded fish were found lying horizontally. Dr Langdon wrote with reference thereto:

> They could not have been placed there by the hand of man, and their position in the layer cannot possibly be explained by any other hypothesis than that of a flood over that part of Mesopotamia. ... When we made these discoveries two months ago we were loth to believe that we had obtained confirmation of the Deluge of Genesis, but there is no doubt about it now.

A still further confirmation of the Biblical story of the Flood from recent archæological discovery is provided

by the Weld-Blundell chronological prism, which is
catalogued WB 444 in the Ashmolean Museum in Oxford.
It is one of a series of tablets purchased in Baghdad.
Professor Langdon, who was the field director of the
expedition which discovered the tablets, says: 'It constitutes
the most important historical document of its kind ever
recovered among cuneiform records.' Its peculiar value
lies in the fact that it was written about the year 2000
BC; that it is a chronological list of ancient Babylonian
kings and dynasties from the beginning of time; that it
refers to the Deluge as making a distinct break in the
succession of those early kings and dynasties; that its
statement 'the Deluge came up', corresponds to the Bible
record that the foundations of the great deep were broken
up, and that something in the nature of a gigantic tidal
wave, besides the continuous rain which came down,
invaded and devastated the earth; and that it shows
conclusively that the ancient Babylonians who lived 4,000
years ago believed in the historicity of the Deluge as surely
as we British believe in the actuality of the Norman
Conquest.

I have written evidentially at this length because of the
need referred to at the beginning of the chapter to
demonstrate the fact that the Noachian Flood, which is
described in three chapters of Genesis, can no longer be
relegated to the limbo of myth or legend or folk-lore;
but that we have there a plain, unvarnished history of an
appalling judgement which was so devastating and so
extensive that it has left its impress in the traditions of
universal mankind.

These traditions extend from China to India and Persia,
from Europe to North and South America, from Central
Africa to Australia and Polynesia. The cuneiform Deluge

tablets, discovered by Mr George Smith of the British Museum in the year 1870, reveal that at a date approximately 3000 BC there was a detailed account of the Flood current in Mesopotamia presenting in a crude, polytheistic form substantially the same story as that related in Genesis, the Biblical story being obviously the pure original.

Mr Catlin, an explorer who has travelled in North, South, and Central America, writes: 'Among the 120 different tribes which I visited, not a tribe exists that has not related to me distinct or vague traditions of such a calamity.' The Moravian missionary, Cranz, in his *History of Greenland*, says that the first missionaries found there a tolerably distinct tradition of the Deluge. Moreover, the Greenlanders themselves point to the remains of fishes and bones of a whale on high mountains where men never could have dwelt, as proof that the earth was once flooded'.[1]

The Chinese tradition is embodied in chaste terms in their book of *Li-Ki:* 'And now the pillars of heaven were broken, the earth shook to its very foundation; the sun and the stars changed their motions; the earth fell to pieces, and the waters enclosed within its bosom burst forth with violence, and overflowed. Man having rebelled against heaven, the system of the universe was totally disordered, and the grand harmony of nature destroyed. All these evils arose from man's despising the supreme power of the universe. He fixed his looks upon terrestrial objects and loved them to excess, until gradually he became transformed into the objects which he loved, and celestial reason abandoned him.'

---

[1] *Contemporary Review,* November, 1879.

Thus the traditional evidence is as overwhelming as the archæological testimony now in our possession. All unprejudiced readers will surely be ready to endorse the verdict of Lenormant, the brilliant French writer of ancient history, who said as far back as 1879: 'As the case now stands, we do not hesitate to declare that, far from being a myth, the Biblical Deluge is a real and historical fact, having, to say the least, left its impress on the ancestors of the three great civilised races of the ancient world, those which constitute the higher humanity—before the ancestors of these races had as yet separated, and in the part of Asia together inhabited.'[1]

## (II) THE NATURE OF THE ANTEDILUVIAN INIQUITY

If we now assume, as I submit we must, that the historicity of the Biblical record of the Flood has been firmly established, we are faced with an enquiry of serious import. What exactly was the nature of the iniquity which occasioned so sweeping a Divine judgement? Having regard to the brevity of the Scriptural narrative, and the vast distance of time which has elapsed, it is a question which it is obvious cannot easily be answered. Concerning this and many other problems of human life in ancient days we know and can know only in part. But sufficient is revealed for our practical guidance in the present and our outlook into the future.

At least one thousand years of human history have intervened since the spotless purity of Eden. During that period there has been a vast increase in population, with

---

[1] *International Standard Bible Encyclopaedia*, Bib. Art. Deluge.

woeful deterioration to a condition of appalling moral corruption. The ultimate origin of this corruption is described in the Genesis story in mysterious terms: 'Now it came to pass, when men began to multiply on the face of the earth, and daughters were born to them, that the sons of God saw the daughters of men, that they were beautiful; and they took wives for themselves of all whom they chose. And the Lord said, "My Spirit shall not strive with man forever, for he is indeed flesh; yet his days shall be one hundred and twenty years." There were giants [Revised Version: Nephilim] on the earth in those days, and also afterward, when the sons of God came in to the daughters of men and they bore children to them. Those were the mighty men who were of old, men of renown' (Genesis 6:1–4).

In this passage there is reference unmistakably to some kind of illicit intercourse between two radically different classes of beings, called the 'sons of God' and the 'daughters of men'. How is this twofold designation to be interpreted? Three very different explanations have been suggested.

First, the 'sons of God' are interpreted by some to be the purely natural descendants of the first man, while the 'daughters of men' are regarded as belonging to a pre-Adamite race which was half bestial in nature. This interpretation appeals to those who incline to think that there was a period in the work of creation when God breathed into a highly developed anthropoid body the 'breath of life', and that man, as we now know him, then emerged. It is the idea which is embodied in Tennyson's phrase, 'The Lord let the house of a beast to the soul of a man'. The illicit intercourse referred to would thus be a union of fully developed men—the sons of God—with women of an undeveloped, semi-brutal, pre-Adamite type.

It need only be added that this suggested explanation creates additional problems; and, moreover, it is one which is entirely destitute of any Scriptural basis.

A second and simpler interpretation is that the union described was just a marriage between the descendants of the first man in the line of Seth, and his descendants in the line of Cain, the former being devoted worshippers of Jehovah, 'Who called upon the name of the Lord', while the latter retained the character and profane instincts of their cursed progenitor. The union which ensued was then simply a contaminating intercourse between the godly and the godless, between the 'converted' and the 'unconverted'. Many modern expositors hold this view. But no sufficient reason exists for the assumption that the descendants of Cain were pre-eminently wicked. One main obstacle in the way of its acceptance lies in the difficulty of accounting for the depth and abnormality of the moral depravity which is so vividly exhibited in the Bible narrative, or how such marriages could produce 'mighty men ... men of renown'.

A third and perhaps more forceful explanation is, that by the 'sons of God' we are to understand fallen angels who somehow entered into illicit intercourse with daughters of men. The advocates of this theory refer to the statement in the 6th and 7th verses of the Epistle of Jude concerning the 'angels who did not keep their proper domain, but left their own abode'. These angels broke bounds; they transgressed, going over the line, forsaking their own legitimate sphere of activity. They are likened accordingly to the men of Sodom and Gomorrah, 'having given themselves over to sexual immorality and gone after strange flesh'. The unnatural sin of the men of Sodom, who burnt with lust towards angels, is thus compared with the unnatural sin of angels who sought illicit association with women. An additional passage which is quoted in support is the statement in 2 Peter 2:4, that 'God did not spare the angels who sinned', made an immediate connexion with the added affirmation in the verse following, that God 'did not spare the ancient world, but saved Noah, one of eight people, a preacher of righteousness, bringing in the flood on the world of the ungodly'.

It is of course common knowledge that stories of unnatural intercourse between deities or demi-gods and the women of mankind, issuing in the production of gigantic and corrupt races, are to be found in the annals of antiquity. Greek mythology abounds in the activities of such heroes and mighty men, of Titans and demi-gods who once flourished in the earth. GH Pember, who is frequently quoted as a strenuous supporter of this theory, writes: 'The children of these unlawful connections before the Flood were the renowned heroes of old: the subsequent repetition of the crime doubtless gave rise to the countless legends of the loves of the gods, and explains the numerous passages in the classics, as well as in the ancient literature of other languages, in which human families are traced to a half divine origin.'[1]

Early Christian expositors, including Justin Martyr, Tertullian, Cyprian, and Ambrose, supported this interpretation. Among scholarly exegetes of recent years it has been maintained by Delitzch, who says in his *New Commentary on Genesis,* that 'we must admit an assumption of human bodies by angels, *i.e.* something in the nature of possession'. He then concludes that 'they were demons who accomplished what is here narrated by means of men whom they made their instruments, *i.e.* through

---

[1] *Earth's Earliest Ages*, p. 212.

demoniacs, who with demoniacal violence drew women within the radius of their enchantments and made them subserve the purpose of their sensual lusts'.

Demon possession is a grim reality. Modern missionaries testify to the awful manifestations of the horrible thing which they have witnessed with their own eyes. In Europe today there are frequent happenings which a multitude of intelligent people do not hesitate to ascribe to the same evil source. If, therefore, the interpretation of Delitzsch, supported as it is by Kurtz, Lenormant, and other distinguished scholars can be justified, we have to understand that fallen angels, leaving their own proper sphere, going after strange flesh, created a race of monsters on earth who were abnormally powerful and devilishly corrupt.

The record adds that 'there were giants in the earth in those days'. But the word 'giants' is not a correct translation of the Hebrew. In the Revised Version we get the original word anglicised in the form Nephilim, which literally means fallen ones. Further, we are told that the offspring of these 'sons of God' and the daughters of men were 'mighty men, the men of renown'.

Altogether an exceedingly dark picture is presented of human depravity. Whatever the precise nature of the foul union which is described, it is certain that the human race in the days of Noah had become very powerful and very profane; arrogant and ruthlessly violent; very big and very bad. Note the terrible indictment: 'The earth also was corrupt before God, and the earth was filled with violence. So God looked upon the earth, and indeed it was corrupt, for all flesh had corrupted their way on the earth' (Genesis 6:11–12).

The Divine decree of world destruction was no sudden pronouncement. The patience of God was long drawn out, both before and during the extended period of the construction of the ark of refuge. But when immense power is allied with extreme wickedness and unspeakable vice, issuing in brute violence of a terrifying order, God, if he be holy, must ultimately intervene. But the sight of it all pained immeasurably the heart of the Eternal. How pathetic is the picture presented in the words, 'Then the LORD saw that the wickedness of man was great in the earth, and that every intent of the thoughts of his heart was only evil continually. And the LORD was sorry that he had made man on the earth, and he was grieved in his heart' (Genesis 6:5–6). Yet, as in the dark tragedy of the Fall, there is a star of hope shining in the night. 'But Noah found grace in the eyes of the LORD.' In one man who walked with God, in one family that had escaped the widespread contamination, the Creator discerns the possibility of a new beginning for the race.

### (III) THE SWEEP OF THE DEVASTATION

The question is often debated: Was the Flood universal in extent, or only partial? The right answer, of course, is that it was universal so far as the race of mankind was concerned. That opinion, however, does not bind us to believe that every square yard of the planet was immersed in the waters of the Deluge. It helps in this connection to remember that the Hebrew word *eretz*, translated 'earth', is also used to signify a district of limited extent. This use of the word is seen in the summons to Abraham: 'Get out of your country *(eretz)*, from your family and from your father's house, to a land (*eretz*) that I will show you' (Genesis 12:1). It also occurs in the address of Pharaoh to Joseph at the time of his elevation to be Prime Minister: 'See, I have set you over all the land (*eretz*) of Egypt' (41:41).

How widespread was the Flood no one knows. It may not have extended far from the district of Mesopotamia, between the rivers Tigris and Euphrates, where the cradle of the race is to be traced, as the Genesis record indicates. Hugh Miller, in his *Testimony of the Rocks,* argued that owing to the shortness of the antediluvian chronology, and the violence and moral corruption of the people, population had not spread beyond the boundary of Western Asia. Alongside that opinion, however, the theory has been presented that, consequent upon the great physical changes in the earth's surface since the closing scenes of the glacial epoch, man had perished from off the face of the earth except in the valley of the Euphrates, and that the Noachian Deluge is the final catastrophe in that series of destructive events. This is not the place to discuss the merits of these opinions. They are dealt with at some length in the article on the Deluge in the *International Standard Bible Encyclopaedia,* by Professor GF Wright, to whom I am greatly indebted. It is interesting to note that he, himself a distinguished geologist, concludes that article with the significant statement: 'It is, therefore, by no means difficult for an all-round geologist to believe in a final catastrophe such as is described in Genesis. If we disbelieve in the Biblical Deluge it is not because we know too much geology, but too little.'

The sweep of the devastation of the Flood, notwithstanding, must have been appallingly vast, as is evidenced by the geological traces which remain, and by the elements of destruction which were brought into operation. It is unfortunately a fallacy widely entertained that the destructiveness of the Deluge was created simply by a forty-days' storm of torrential rain, and that after the forty days had expired all was over. Those who cling to this misconception are apt to receive a shock when they discover that the Deluge was so vast and so all-embracing, that Noah and his family were incarcerated in the ark of preservation for a period exceeding a whole year.

In what the late Sir William Dawson, the distinguished Canadian geologist, described as 'Noah's Log Book', contained in Genesis 7:7 to 8:19, it is revealed that Noah and his family entered the ark on the 17th day of the second month, and that they emerged therefrom on the 27th day of the same month in the year following, making the total period of the judgement no less than 370 days! Though the downfall of the rain continued for only forty days, the Bible records that the waters continued to prevail thereafter for 150 days; and further, before they had sufficiently subsided, another 150 days had to elapse.

We know now that the prolonged period of incarceration in the ark was necessitated by the terrific violence of the elements which brought about the vast catastrophe. They were twofold in character. The 'windows of heaven' were opened, and a cataract of rain descended during forty nights and days. But the second and more powerful agent which operated was that described in the words: 'on that day all the fountains of the great deep were broken up' (Genesis 7:11).

A cataclysm somewhat of the nature of an earthquake, with an extensive cracking of the earth's crust appears to be indicated, so that the waters of the ocean overwhelmed the land with terrific energy. Science reveals that intense heat occurs immediately below the surface of our planet. Volcanic activity is one of its commonest manifestations; the occurrence of hot springs is another. We have therefore only to imagine a series of gigantic cracks in the ground surface of the ocean, with a correspondingly immense escape of the heat which lies beneath, producing enormous outbursts of steam of immeasurable velocity, to realise how vastly different was the cataclysm of the Flood from the mere rain-storm of forty days of the popular imagination. To the torrential downrush from the clouds was added the gigantic uprush from the ocean; so that the waters prevailed or dominated the earth during one hundred and fifty days; and therefore, as so precisely detailed, another one hundred and fifty days had to elapse before the elect family could be safely released from the place of preservation wherein they had waited upon the providence of God.

According to Professor Wright, the breaking up of 'the fountains of the great deep' might be interpreted as 'phenomena connected with one of the downward movements of the earth's crust with which geology has made us familiar. The sinking of the land below the level of the ocean is equivalent, in its effects, to the rising of the water above it, and is accurately expressed by the phrases used in the sacred narrative.'[1] Whether that be so, certain it is that something in the nature of tidal waves of cosmic magnitude, overwhelming the land surface of the earth, greatly contributed to the terrifying catastrophe. And it is interesting to note in connection

---

[1] *Op. cit.*

with this mighty overflow of the waters of the ocean, that the ark sailed not southwards towards the sea, but northwards into the interior of the land, and finally rested on the highlands of Ararat, situated somewhere in the territory of Armenia.

## (iv) THE TYPICAL SIGNIFICANCE OF THE CATASTROPHE

The first eleven chapters of Genesis constitute an extremely condensed historic record. How few realise when they have reached the end of the eleventh chapter that they have already traversed more than one half of the historic time recorded in the whole Bible. In those early chapters, to turn over a single page may be equivalent to the passing over of half a millennium. So the story of the Flood is not far removed in the sacred literature from the inspired record of the Creation. This arrangement may easily confuse the careless reader. But one distinct value can be discerned in this close contiguity. The earnest Bible student meets thus early in the sacred volume a warning light for all the subsequent ages of mankind, in the catastrophic ending of a dispensation, by an appalling devastation which overtook the monstrous race of men then living, because of the foulness of their iniquity. Later he will discover that the Son of God, in the days of his flesh, predicted that that cataclysm would prove to be a type of an even more awful catastrophe which would signalise the end of the present age of the earth and mankind.

How simple yet how solemn were the Master's prophetic words, especially when rendered with the force of the original Greek: 'As it was in the days of Noah so it will be also in the days of the Son of Man. They were completely absorbed in eating, and drinking, and marrying, and giving in marriage, until the day that Noah entered the ark and the flood came and destroyed them all. Likewise as it was also in the days of Lot, they were given up to eating, and drinking, and buying, and selling, and planting, and building. But in the same day that Lot went out of Sodom it rained fire and brimstone from heaven, and destroyed them all. After the same manner shall it be in the day when the Son of man is revealed' (Luke 17:26–30).

No promise there of constant improvement in the moral and spiritual condition of mankind; no prediction of a perpetual advance towards a high ideal; no foolish anticipation of the inevitability of progress—that ridiculous obsession of the nineteenth century! Rather did the Master warn his disciples of the approach of a great apostasy especially towards the end of the age—when wars and rumours of war would be rife; when the love of many would wax cold, and faithful disciples would be few but persecutions would be many; when the true Church would become but a remnant in the midst of an alienated world intent upon merely materialistic interests and pursuits, having lost the vision of God and of the things eternal. So dark is the prospect that the divine Lord is compelled to ask in dread anticipation, 'when the Son of Man comes, will he really find faith on the earth' (Luke 18:8)?

Is it hard to discern such 'signs of the times' in our own day and generation? What do we see immediately around us? What is the characteristic of the generality of human kind known to us? Is it not such preoccupation with the things of time and sense and the transitory affairs of this life that the claims of Almighty God upon the soul are utterly ignored? Materialism and sensuality, scepticism and unbelief, religious declension and apostasy, greed and godlessness, superstitious devotion to the cults of spiritism and astrology; and all these wedded to low moral corruption, violence and brutality unparalleled, are conspicious features of modern life, especially in the countries of Europe which have been most highly favoured in the past with the light of the holy Gospel of the grace of God. Instead of a civilisation we had hoped to see Christianised, we are confronted by the dread spectre of a civilisation becoming completely paganised. Because of the taint of moral leprosy which no one absolutely escapes, human nature, left to itself, devoid of the regenerating grace of the Holy Spirit, does not tend to rise upwards, but always to slide downwards to things 'earthly, sensual, demonic'.

At a moment swift and sudden, when least expected, the judgement at the end of the age will begin to operate. And the final catastrophe will be as appallingly universal in its scope as the first. To the question: Where Lord? in what part of the earth will it take place? the Master returned an answer which was as pregnant as it was brief: 'wherever the carcass is, there the eagles will be gathered together' (Matthew 24:28). It was a grim Eastern proverb. The scene which it presents is somewhat like this. A caravan is crossing the desert. One of the camels sickens, gets worse, and finally falls down dead. The caravan moves on, leaving the carcase behind. The sky is an unbroken blue. Not a cloud is to be seen. But, after a while, some dark spots appear in the sky, growing larger and coming nearer. It is a flock of vultures. By some rare instinct of sight or smell they have become aware of a rotting carcase lying on the desert sand. Down they swoop upon the carrion, fighting fiercely with flapping wings to get near to rend the flesh with their strong talons, crowding around the fallen beast for the hideous meal until not a morsel of meat remains. So shall it be in that great Day! Everywhere, in every place, wherever men and women are living lives of godlessness and moral corruption with contempt for God's Word and Commandment, there will the sweep of the divine judgement operate, and not one soul shall escape.

### (v) BUT NOAH: ARE THERE FEW THAT BE SAVED?

'But Noah found grace in the eyes of the Lord.' For Noah was a righteous man; he walked with God; he had learned to live upon the higher plane of divine communion and fellowship. So a tiny remnant is provided whereby God can initiate a new movement in the realm of mankind. Only eight persons; but they sufficed. Thus early in the Bible we discover the divine principle of the remnant—found illustrated from Genesis to Revelation—that the Almighty God is ever working towards the fulfilment of his gracious purposes for the future through the instrumentality of a selected few.

In the light of our Lord's clear prediction concerning the end of the age, the question spontaneously arises: Are there few that be saved? How did the Master answer when thus confronted? We discover that he resolved the problem after a manner which was sublimely practical. He said in effect: You take this home into your inmost heart. Your supreme business is not to speculate. but to strive. Strive to enter into the Kingdom (the Greek word is literally *agonise*). Concentrate all your energies until it costs to make your calling and election sure; for 'broad is the way that leads to destruction, and there are many who go in by it. Because narrow is the gate and difficult is the way which leads to life, and there are few who find it' (Matthew 7:13–14).

In all our churches and denominations there is an unsaved multitude who are loosely attached to the organisation, having no living contact with the Lord who is the divine head of a mystical body. Such need to ponder the question addressed by a devout Sunday School superintendent to the worldly-minded young man who acted as his school librarian: 'Have you ever thought what became of Noah's carpenters?'

Christendom covers a vast area; true Christians are few and far between. And why? What is the fundamental reason? It is non-compliance with the primary direction of Jesus Christ to all who desire to follow him: 'Seek! Seek first!' Let God and the interests of the immortal soul occupy the proper place of pre-eminence in your heart and life. If you do you will find that all other things that are needful will be added. Blessed are they that obey Christ's precept. For the promise holds, 'If with all your heart ye seek the Lord, ye shall surely find him'; and, finding him, the divine Redeemer, will enter into a sure ark of preservation and salvation in the time of storm.

## Chapter 2

# SODOM AND GOMORRAH: EXTERMINATION OF THE SODOMITES AND CANAANITES

And the Lord said, 'Because the outcry against Sodom and Gomorrah is great, and because their sin is very grave, I will go down now and see whether they have done altogether according to the outcry against it that has come to me; and if not, I will know.'

Now the two angels came to Sodom in the evening, and Lot was sitting in the gate of Sodom. When Lot saw them, he rose to meet them, and he bowed himself with his face toward the ground.

When the morning dawned, the angels urged Lot to hurry, saying, 'Arise, take your wife and your two daughters who are here, lest you be consumed in the punishment of the city.' And while he lingered, the men took hold of his hand, his wife's hand, and the hands of his two daughters, the Lord being merciful to him, and they brought him out and set him outside the city.

Then the Lord rained brimstone and fire on Sodom and Gomorrah, from the Lord out of the heavens. So he overthrew those cities, all the plain, all the inhabitants of the cities, and what grew on the ground. But his wife looked back behind him, and she became a pillar of salt. And Abraham went early in the morning to the place where he had stood before the Lord. Then he looked toward Sodom and Gomorrah, and toward all the land of the plain; and he saw, and behold, the smoke of the land which went up like the smoke of a furnace. (Genesis 18:20, 21; 19:1, 15–16, 24–28).

A COMMERCIAL company called *Palestine Potash Limited,* whose registered office was then at 62 Pall Mall, London, S.W., published a few years ago a prospectus entitled 'The Dead Sea Chemical Industry'. In that interesting compilation, which describes the production for commercial purposes of the valuable chemical constituents of the Dead Sea—potassium chloride, magnesium bromide, etc.—the following statement occurs in its opening page: 'The Dead Sea owes its origin to one of the oldest cosmic catastrophes known to mankind. That catastrophe is described in the Biblical story of Sodom and Gomorrah which, in our childhood, impressed us with an image of dread and terror and the curse of hell. Geological evidence, accumulated during centuries and derived from numerous scientific expeditions, to a large extent substantiates that Biblical account.'

Thus an ancient Biblical record, the truth of which has been severely challenged, receives confirmation today from an unexpected source. And this testimony does not stand alone.

## (1) THE FACT SCIENTIFICALLY ESTABLISHED

Less than twenty years ago an expedition was formed to explore the whole territory with the object of testing the accuracy of the Biblical narrative. The result was a remarkable corroboration of the record down to some of its minutest details.

The party was a representative one. The President was Dr Melvin Grove Kyle, a Presbyterian, of the Xenia Theological Seminary, Missouri, USA. It included Dr Albright, a Methodist, of the American School of Oriental Research at Jerusalem, and Mr Makhouli, of the Department of Antiquities, a member of the Greek Catholic Church in Palestine. The leading archæologist was Père Mallon, a Jesuit priest of Jerusalem; the geologist was Professor Alfred Day, of the Beirut College in Syria. In addition to several scholarly assistants, the expedition profited by the advice of Mr Dunsmore, of Jerusalem, reputed to be the most expert botanist in Palestine, and the judgement of Père Vincent, the foremost Palestinian scholar in the world.

Among the manifold results of the investigations, which were conducted in a strictly scientific manner, the following are of particular interest and value.

First, the Bible description of the original beauty and fertility of the district was confirmed. In Genesis 13, when Abraham and Lot agreed to separate so as to divide the pasture lands between their flocks, it is recorded that Lot 'lifted his eyes and saw all the plain of Jordan, that it was well watered everywhere (before the Lord destroyed Sodom and Gomorrah) *like the garden of the Lord'.* So Lot, it is added, 'chose for himself all the plain of Jordan ... Lot dwelt in the cities of the plain and pitched his tent even as far as Sodom.' Dr Kyle, as the result of a careful and protracted survey, was impressed by the salubrious climate of the district, its tropical luxuriousness, the excellent water springing from the red sandstone of Moab, its romantic scenery, and the possibility of its becoming one of the finest winter resorts in the world.

Secondly, it has been established that the elements of destruction in the vast upheaval were undoubtedly such as the Scripture represents. in a volume entitled *Explorations at Sodom,* Dr Kyle testifies that

> the great catastrophe did take place exactly as narrated in the Bible. ... This region was found by the geologists to be a burnt-out region of oil and ashphalt, of which material, indeed, there is again an accumulation that will soon be exploited. ... Now wherever these conditions exist there is an accumulation of gases, and the geologists tell us that here, at some time which they cannot exactly fix, these gases were ignited by some means, also to them unknown, and there was a great explosion, with first an upheaval, and then a subsidence of the strata. The character of the ruptured strata has also been determined, with most interesting conclusions. There is along the lower part of the plain a great stratum of rock-salt, which on the western side of the plain shows itself in that great salt mountain now known as Jebel Usdum. At its base is a stratum of rock-salt about one hundred and fifty feet thick. It is almost pure salt, but lies in layers of varying thickness. Mixed with the layers of salt, and falling down over them also, is a marl in which is much free sulphur, lumps of which we picked up along the sea. When the explosion of the gases took place, this stratum of salt mixed with sulphur was ruptured with the other strata, and the salt and sulphur carried up into the heavens red-hot, and so rained down upon Sodom and Gomorrah and over the whole region exactly as the Scripture describes.[1]

---

[1] P. 128–130.

Thirdly, there is evidence in abundance to illustrate the scene as it must have presented itself to an eye-witness. Professor G Frederick Wright, of Oberlin College, Oberlin, Ohio, a distinguished American geologist, familiar with the oil-gas regions of the United States, went over the ground about the end of nineteenth century, and took away the impression that the secondary causes which produced the catastrophe were the ignition of vast subterranean deposits of petroleum and gas by volcanic agency. That asphalt or bitumen was widespread in the district thousands of years ago is evidenced by the fact that both Pliny and Josephus called the Dead Sea 'Lake Asphaltites'. In the gigantic conflagration which ensued, sulphur, salt and asphalt would be heated to a tremendously high degree. A dense smoke screen would certainly be created. Dr Kyle pertinently asks: 'What makes a greater smoke than a vat of boiling asphalt at work on the street?'[1]

Abraham, at the time of the catastrophe, was still at Hebron, about sixteen miles away. But, standing on one of the heights in his vicinity, he could look eastwards through a gap in the hills to the great depression of the plain, which lay four thousand feet below. What he actually saw is thus recorded: 'And Abraham went early in the morning to the place where he had stood before the Lord. Then he looked toward Sodom and Gomorrah, and toward all the land of the plain; and he saw, and behold, the smoke of the land which went up like the smoke of a furnace' (Genesis 19:27–28).

Fourthly, the precise location of the cities of the plain— formerly a disputed point—has been fixed at the southern end of the Dead Sea. In *The Deciding Voice of the Monuments*, Professor Kyle writes: 'The rising of the Dead Sea since

---

[1] *Op. cit.*, p. 130.

the days of Abraham, by reason of the filling in of the
delta of the Jordan at the north end, has resulted in the
sea running over at the southern edge and flooding the
plain. There, in a few feet of water and mud, the ruined
cities hide their shame. The High Place and the cemetery
of their noble dead, being upon higher ground, is still
to be seen.'[1] That a civilisation such as that represented
in the Bible story undoubtedly existed at the time has
been established. Moreover, the evidence is convincing
that such a civilisation abruptly ceased. 'The most careful
search of the plain from one end to the other, with
soundings down to virgin sand and gravel ... showed that
from about 1800 BC on to the end of the Biblical period,
there was no civilisation of any kind on the Plain. This
exactly coincides with the silence of Biblical history from
the destruction of the cities onward. Here is one instance
when negative evidence became positive.[2]

Finally, the possibility of such a fate as that which befell
Lot's wife is circumstantiated by what still remains in the
neighbourhood of the buried cities. 'A great rock-salt
stratum exposed six miles in length and 150 feet thick;
free sulphur which lies over the plain now and mingles
with the marl which overlies the salt, teach exactly the
location of the tragedy.' Fire and bituminous smoke, salt
and burning sulphur, would quickly operate to destroy
life and fertility. What goes up comes down. Thus the
raining down of 'brimstone and fire on Sodom and
Gomorrah, from the Lord out of the heavens' is the
striking imagery of the Biblical narrative describing what
actually occurred. And this was accompanied by a deluge
of finely powdered salt, descending and enveloping like

---

[1] P. 255.

[2] *Op. cit.*, p. 254.

a fierce snow-drift. So it came to pass that Lot's wife, probably lusting after treasures left behind in Sodom, lingered, and while she lingered she was blinded and suffocated by the dense, sulphurous smoke. In her helplessness, becoming quickly overwhelmed, she was encrusted from head to foot by the saline deposit descending thickly upon her, so that where she stood she was transformed into 'a pillar of salt'. The mountain peaks which to this day are capped with salt, provide a perpetual reminder of the awful fate which befell one who hesitated and halted when she should have surrendered herself to the angel guardianship which was close at hand. Quite reasonably does Dr Kyle sum up the result of his researches in the words, 'the geologists have found in nature exactly what the Biblical record describes in Providence'.

## (II) THE REASON SCRIPTURALLY PRESENTED

Next to the judgement of the Flood in the days of Noah, the most terrible act of divine punishment of the wicked recorded in the Old Testament, is that of the destruction of the Cities of the Plain. Our divine Lord placed the seal of his imprimatur upon its historical character in severe words of condemnation of the faithless, unbelieving towns which bordered the Sea of Galilee. 'And you, Capernaum, who are exalted to heaven, will be brought down to Hades; for if the mighty works which were done in you had been done in Sodom, it would have remained until this day' (Matthew 11:23).

The reason for the appalling act of judgement which fell upon the cities of the plain is clearly revealed. Earlier in the Genesis record than the actual story of the cataclysm, at a period at least twenty years before, it is stated that 'the men of Sodom were exceedingly wicked and sinful against the Lord' (Genesis 13:13). In the language of Isaiah (Isaiah 3:9) they 'declared' their sin; they took no pains to conceal it; it was blatant and brazenly exhibited; for they had lost all sense of shame.

But before the guilty cities meet their doom, an angelic visitation of enquiry of an exceedingly august character, is graphically depicted. Three heavenly messengers suddenly appear before Abraham at Hebron. The purpose of the visit is manifest—the final test of Sodom. A careful comparison of the various Scriptural statements here is helpful. In the first verse it is said, 'The *Lord* appeared to him'; in the next verse it is said that *'Three men* were standing by him'. But one of the three is obviously of outstanding noble and dignified appearance; for in the third verse Abraham, ignoring as it were the presence of the other two, addresses him only, saying, 'My Lord, if I have now found favour in your sight, do not pass on by your servant'.

Though they appear in human form, Abraham, presently, though not immediately, recognises their supernatural character. For a space at least he 'unwittingly entertained angels'; not discerning the heavenly origin of his visitors. One of the three is greatly distinguished from the outset. Though addressed as 'My Lord' at the first, merely as an Eastern salutation of respectful courtesy such as might ordinarily be given to an honoured guest, it is evident in the intercourse which followed, that his divine character is clearly recognised. This is seen in the tokens of profound reverence and obeisance, which later characterises the behaviour of the patriarch throughout.

The two ministers of vengeance who are called men in chapter 18 are described as angels in the opening verse of chapter 19. Soon they depart to go on their way to Sodom. After their departure we read that Abraham 'still stood before *the* Lord' in an attitude of worship and *earnest intercession*, pleading his pathetic prayer for the preservation of Sodom, even if only ten righteous men might be found therein. It appears, therefore, from this and corresponding passages, that we have here recorded a Theophany of the Son of God—the Angel of the Lord— a manifestation on the earth of him who in the fullness of time became incarnate for the purpose of the redemption of mankind. He was not merely an angel, but the Lord of the angels. It may well be that this visit is embraced in the mysteriously significant declaration of Jesus Christ spoken to the Jews in the days of his flesh: 'Your father Abraham rejoiced to see my day, and he saw it and was glad' (John 8:56).

As we picture the horrible desolation brought upon the earth by this direct act of God, it is of pre-eminent importance to note the meticulous care which was taken to examine the evidence before the final verdict was pronounced. Judgement was preceded by painstaking enquiry, conducted by messengers of the Most High. For it is written: 'And the Lord said, "Because the outcry against Sodom and Gomorrah is great, and because their sin is very grave, I will go down now and see whether they have done altogether according to the outcry against it that has come to me; and if not, I will know"' (Genesis 18:20–21). In his visitations God never acts precipitately, but with absolute justice, and only after perfect knowledge of all that can conduce to a righteous judgement.

When the angels of the divine wrath arrive at Sodom, they are met by Lot at the city gate. What follows is vividly portrayed. It all culminates in an exhibition of such unspeakably bestial abomination that no additional evidence was required; no further witness need be called.

Cordially welcomed by Lot in true Oriental fashion, received as honoured guests into his house, and freely offered the privileges of gracious hospitality, they prepared to spend the night resting quietly under his roof. But the peace of the household is suddenly disturbed. The attention of the inhabitants has been drawn to the arrival of these distinguished visitors. Probably there was, as Josephus supposes, a beauty and dignity about their persons, corresponding to their exalted character and mission, which, instead of creating enhanced respect seems to have awakened only depraved passions and carnal lusts in the hearts of the citizens of a city which had become notorious by its detestable vices.

A fierce clamouring at the door is accompanied by insistent demands that the strangers to the city, who are the guests of Lot, shall be put out into the street, for an unspeakably vile purpose. The stratagem which Lot attempted in order to induce them to desist from their detestable purpose, condescending even to permit his own daughters to descend into the lowest pit of immoral degradation, serves only to illustrate horribly the extreme corruption of the guilty city.

Straightway the divine decree is put into execution; the verdict of High Heaven takes immediate effect. Measures for the safety of Lot and the members of his family are counselled by the avenging angels, who then explicitly announce the immediacy of the impending judgement:

'For we will destroy this place, because the outcry against them has grown great before the face of the Lord, and the Lord has sent us to destroy it' (Genesis 19:13).

Sodom! The name has become a synonym of vile corruption. No less than thirty times Sodom is referred to in the Holy Scriptures as a gross example of human iniquity, and a perpetual monument of the avenging wrath of God, when kindled by the utterly unbridled passions of the wicked. Surely, in the fight of all the facts, no defence is required to justify this devastating act of the hand of the Almighty. The case has been presented by a powerful Scriptural exegete of a past generation so trenchantly, yet so justly, that I cannot forbear to quote his weighty words, which evoke my profoundest assent.

> Given a city that is full of corruption which may not be so much as named; every home a den of unclean beasts; every imagination debauched and drunk with iniquity; every tongue an empoisoned instrument; purity, love, honour, peace, forgotten or detested words: judgement deposed, righteousness banished, the sanctuary abandoned, the altar destroyed; every child taught the trick and speech of imps; prizes offered for the discovery of some deeper depth of iniquity or new way of serving the devil—given such a city, to know what is best to be done with it? *Remonstrate* with it? Absurd! *Threaten* it? Feeble! What then? *Rain fire and brimstone upon it?* Yes! Conscience says Yes; justice says Yes; concern for other cities says Yes; nothing but fire will disinfect so foul an air, nothing but burning brimstone should succeed the cup of devils. Just as we grasp the moral condition with which God had to deal do we see that fire alone could meet wickedness so wicked or insanity so mad.[1]

---

[1] Parker, *The People's Bible*, Vol. i., p. 224.

## (III) THE PURPOSE PROGRESSIVELY REVEALED

The Cities of the Plain which were so utterly destroyed were not merely two, but four. In a warning message given to Israel by Moses at the time of the Exodus, he refers to the appalling historic devastation in these terms: 'The whole land thereof is brimstone and salt, and burning ... like the overthrow of Sodom and Gomorrah, Admah and Zeboim, which the Lord overthrew in his anger, and in his wrath' (Deuteronomy 29:23). If we include the small town of Zoar which was plainly implicated, there was a Pentapolis of guilty cities in the vale of Siddim. Sodom, apparently, was just the largest and most infamous of the lot.

Now there is abundant evidence to show that these five cities of the Jordan Plain were representative of the low moral condition of ancient Canaan. They were not alone in their iniquity. The vile men of Sodom who besieged the house of Lot, were, the Scripture says, 'both old and young, all the people from every quarter, surrounded the house'. This widespread shamelessness and unbridled licentiousness of one city so flagrantly expressed, may be regarded as a sample of the widespread impiety and immorality which were characteristic of that ancient Canaan which was divinely indicated to be a Land of Promise, to become a centre of spiritual light and life for all the nations of mankind. The same lasciviousness linked with idolatry of a very degraded character predominated and prevailed. So that the extermination of the Canaanites in the days of Joshua, which is so severely criticised by many today, belongs to the same category as that of the destruction of the Cities of the Plain.

In the charge of Moses, delivered to the people of Israel at the end of their long desert journey, on the borders of the Promised Land, he refers distinctly to the moral degradation of the Canaanites, who were then in possession, in these prophetic terms: 'because of the wickedness of these nations that the Lord is driving them out from before you. It is not because of your righteousness or the uprightness of your heart that you go in to possess their land, but because of the wickedness of these nations that the Lord your God drives them out from before you, and that he may fulfil the word which the Lord swore to your fathers, to Abraham, Isaac, and Jacob' (Deuteronomy 9:4–5).

Recent archæology has substantiated the charge which Israel's emancipator and law-giver then pronounced. Human sacrifice was prevalent. Professor RAS Macalister, who conducted archæological investigations at Gezer, one of the ancient Canaanitish cities, between 1902 and 1909, unearthed convincing proofs of this revolting rite. He says that the whole area of the High Place was found to be a cemetery of new-born infants. These infants were deposited in large jars, some showing marks of having passed through the fire.

One of the pits at Gezer contained the skeleton of a young girl sawn in half, together with two decapitated skeletons, and the upper half of a skeleton of a boy. A monstrous religious custom especially prevalent was the so-called foundation sacrifice. Quite frequently an earthenware jar, containing the bones of an infant, is found beneath the foundation pillars of a building. Traces of a living child being thus entombed have been revealed. The idea presumably was that the life and vitality of the child would become part of the edifice, ensuring its stability. Such a sacrifice is undoubtedly referred to when we read that in the days of Ahab, 'Hiel of Bethel built Jericho', and that 'he laid its foundation with [the loss of, KJV] Abiram his firstborn' (1 Kings 16:34).

A principal object of worship was Ashtoreth, 'the name of the supreme goddess of Canaan and the female counterpart of Baal'. The name and cult of the goddess were derived from ancient Babylonia, where she was worshipped under the name of Istar. There prostitution was practised in her name; and her worship was regularly associated with immoral rites by bands of both men and women. According to Professor Sayce, 'the immoral rites with which the worship of Istar in Babylonia was accompanied were transferred to Canaan (Deuteronomy 23:18), and formed part of the idolatrous practices which the Israelites were called upon to extirpate'.[1] Herodotus has borne testimony to this mark of Canaanitish degradation; and the blighting influence of this heathen cult upon the spiritual life of Israel is repeatedly referred to in the Scriptural history of God's chosen people. Quite early in the Book of Judges it is recorded that 'they followed other gods from among the gods of the people who were all around them, and they bowed down to them; and they provoked the Lord to anger. They forsook the Lord and served Baal and the Ashtoreths' (Judges 2:12–13).[2]

Here, then, with reverence be it said, was the problem which presented itself before the eyes of the Lord, who sees the end from the beginning—drastic extermination or continuous contamination? Should he permit the exceedingly low moral and religious condition of the

---

[1] *Vide* Art. 'Ashtoreth' in *International Standard Bible Encyclopædia*.

[2] Ashtaroth, plural of Ashtoreth.

Canaanites to continue unchecked, allowing an elect
nation to enter into their midst with the certainty of their
being corrupted, thus frustrating his purposes of blessing
for the whole of mankind; or should he take steps to
destroy the foul contagion, by decreeing the removal of
an unclean minority in order to preserve the moral and
spiritual purity of a vast majority of the sons and daughters
of men?

The decision which the Almighty God reached is not
in doubt. It is revealed in the explicit directions, oft
repeated, which he gave through Moses, and again through
Joshua, his successor: 'When the Lord your God brings
you into the land which you go to possess, and has cast
out many nations before you … and when the Lord your
God delivers them over to you, you shall conquer them
and utterly destroy them. You shall make no covenant
with them nor show mercy to them. Nor shall you make
marriages with them. … For they will turn your sons away
from following me, to serve other gods … But thus you
shall deal with them: you shall destroy their altars, and
break down their sacred pillars, and cut down their
wooden images, and burn their carved images with fire'
(Deuteronomy 7:1–5).

Now this is one of those Scriptural records which
provokes the severe denunciation of certain modern
critics, including not a few ordained clergy who have
professed vows of allegiance to the complete Canon of
Holy Scripture. In a Scottish city not long ago, a minister
of the Church of Scotland stirred a high degree of
resentment in the hearts of his brethren, at a meeting
of the Provincial Sunday School, by fiercely condemning
the teaching of the Old Testament to the children,
describing it as in part 'morally pernicious'. 'Must we fill

the mind of the child,' he asked, 'with a conception of God as a jealous, and vindictive, and bloodthirsty tyrant, who could do nothing better than order the slaughter of women and children to appease his wrath?'

Apparently it had never dawned upon the speaker's consciousness that the only Bible the boy Jesus had, out of which his mother taught him, and the only Bible which Paul possessed when, as a student of the Law, he sat at the feet of Gamaliel, and the only Bible out of which Stephen at his martyrdom made his defence, his face meantime shining like the face of an angel, was this same collection of the oracles of God called the Old Testament, which this modern ministerial denunciator demands shall be taken out of the hands of the children of the Christian Church.

Fiery declamation such as this, however, only amounts to practically verbatim reproduction of utterances which represent the stock-in-trade of infidelity down the centuries. But, notwithstanding these bitter attacks, there are in our midst tens of thousands of devout Christian parents who will gladly, yea, eagerly, place the Old Testament Scriptures into the hands of their offspring from their infancy, preferring that their children should become acquainted thereby with the dark and sordid side of human life and conduct, rather than through the medium of the typical modern novel featuring its ever recurring sex problem *ad nauseam*, or the glamorous cinema play generally so far removed from the grim, grey actualities of daily life.

But the best answer to such crude criticism as that represented above is summed up in the proverbial saying *respice finem*. Contemplate the acts of God recorded, not as isolated incidents, but as part of a magnificent plan of regeneration and renewal, gradually unfolding, stretching across the centuries, beginning with the call of Abraham, proceeding through Moses and the prophets towards its glorious culmination and consummation in Christ—coming at the first as a Saviour to redeem, and coming again as a Sovereign to reign—all to inaugurate and make real the golden period of the long-promised Kingdom of God upon the earth.

It is of great significance that before the destruction of Sodom was determined, we are told that Abraham, 'the friend of God', was taken into the counsels of the Most High, who revealed to him in some measure the divine plans and purposes for the future. He was initiated into certain mysteries in the mind of God. 'And the Lord said, "Shall I hide from Abraham what I am doing, since Abraham shall surely become a great and mighty nation, and all the nations of the earth shall be blessed in him?"' (Genesis 18:17–18). The destruction of Sodom was not a mere exhibition of the wrath of God in his dealings with sinful men. It was much more the removal of an immense obstacle which blocked the way towards a divinely predestined goal for the race.

The Hebrews provide the key to history. Their preservation is the outstanding miracle of the ages; a miracle explainable only by the fact that they were called to be an elect nation for the fulfilment of high and holy purposes, embracing the whole race of mankind, according to the original promise made to their father Abraham: 'I will make you a great nation; I will bless you and make your name great … and in you all the families of the earth shall be blessed' (Genesis 12:2–3).

This purpose of God has been progressively revealed throughout the ages—a purpose which even we can see

in part fulfilled. Godet, the eminent Swiss divine of the
last century, who combined in an exceptional degree ripe
scholarship with rare spiritual insight, has emphasised
this cardinal truth in weighty words:

> Rome saw in foreign nations only material for her triumph;
> but Israel, from the very beginning, looked upon itself as
> the agent for the salvation of the world, as the predestined
> instrument for the welfare of the nations. This marvellous
> fact deserves more serious attention from the philosophy
> of history than it has yet received. … Whilst we see all other
> nations marching forward with gaze fixed upon the earth,
> and absorbed only in thoughts of their own power and
> temporal prosperity, Israel is seen, in history, advancing
> with hands ever outstretched towards a future good, distinctly
> contemplated, and the hope of which it boldly makes the
> very principle and support of its existence.[1]

Thus, when this chosen people under the leadership of
Joshua were about to enter the land of promise, it became
a matter of pre-eminent importance, if they were to fulfil
their high destiny to be 'a light to bring revelation to the
Gentiles', that they should have as pure an environment,
and a habitation as free from contamination, as could
possibly be provided. They were to be a people separated
and consecrated unto the Lord; fit recipients of revelation
from on high; and centrally situated in the earth, so as
to become a source of spiritual life and of the knowledge
of the true God unto all the nations of mankind. 'For
you are a holy people to the Lord your God; the Lord
your God has chosen you to be a people for himself, a
special treasure above all the peoples on the face of the
earth' (Deuteronomy 7:6).

Yet, notwithstanding all the care and forethought divinely
bestowed, Israel lapsed again and again into the gross

---

[1] *Studies in the Old Testament*, p. 140.

idolatries and the lascivious rites of the Canaanites with whom they came in contact in the covenanted land. The degeneracy which ensued is clearly traceable, as their prophets testified, to their slackness or unwillingness to extirpate their idolatrous neighbours, as they had been explicitly commanded. Evil communications corrupt and contaminate. Thus after seven centuries had run their course since Israel first entered Canaan, Isaiah, the prince of the prophets, can only fitly describe them as 'a people laden with iniquity, a brood of evildoers, children who are corrupters! They have forsaken the Lord' (Isaiah 1:4). Israel is then on the edge of a precipice; its fall is imminent. Only the presence of a faithful few prevented its entire collapse, as the prophet confesses: 'Unless the Lord of hosts had left to us a very small remnant, we would have become like Sodom, we would have been made like Gomorrah' (Isaiah 1:9).

Later, in the 106th Psalm, the sad picture of Israel's declension is mournfully presented and the cause bluntly indicated: 'They did not destroy the peoples, concerning whom the Lord had commanded them, but they mingled with the Gentiles and learned their works; they served their idols, which became a snare to them. They even sacrificed their sons and their daughters to demons, and shed innocent blood, the blood of their sons and daughters, whom they sacrificed to the idols of Canaan; and the land was polluted with blood. Thus they were defiled by their own works, and played the harlot by their own deeds' (Psalm 106:34–39).

Finally, after the people of Israel themselves had experienced the horrors of a ravaged and a desolated land, and all but the poorest were transported across the desert into Babylon, the land of their predicted captivity,

Ezekiel, the eagle-eyed prophet, brings to their remembrance there the foul record of national sin and apostasy which had caused their downfall, rebuking the spiritual harlotry of Jerusalem, tracing the iniquity of God's elect people backwards to its foul taproot in Sodom. 'Again the word of the Lord came to me, saying, "Son of man, cause Jerusalem to know her abominations, and say, 'Thus says the Lord God to Jerusalem: "Your birth and your nativity are from the land of Canaan … Look, this was the iniquity of your sister Sodom: she and her daughter had pride, fullness of food, and abundance of idleness; neither did she strengthen the hand of the poor and needy. And they were haughty and committed abomination before me; therefore I took them away as I saw fit"'"' (Ezekiel 16:1–3, 49–50).

'Surgery not butchery!' That is how a scholarly and spiritually-minded doctor of divinity summed up the solution of the problem, when I discussed it with him one day walking together on the famous Braid Hills in Edinburgh. The distinction needs to be clearly recognised. A man is brought into the Royal Infirmary, wounded or diseased in a particular limb. After a skilful examination by a surgeon of high repute the verdict is pronounced in one word: Amputation! In order to preserve, the life and vitality of the man's body, his diseased limb must be cut off.

Down the ages, in order to safeguard the physical vigour and the moral integrity of the whole body of the human race, certain incurable, corrupt, and contagious portions have had to be cut away. God has had no other alternative. He has decreed extermination for the purpose of preservation—extermination of the filthy for the preservation and purification of the fit—for the service of God in the highest interests of mankind. Someone has said: 'What the history of our world would have been if that hotbed of Canaanite corruption had continued, it would be difficult to imagine.'

Therefore, to represent him as a bloodthirsty and vindictive tyrant, in the fashion so commonly current today is, I do not hesitate to describe, a gross caricature of the character of Jehovah, the Holy One of Israel. Not a single page of the Old Testament substantiates such a charge. It could not survive save as the buttress of a theory of the evolutionary ascent of religion from animism to polytheism, and polytheism to monotheism—a theory now hopelessly discredited by the scientific facts brought to light in the realm of philology and archæology. A God of judgement Jehovah undoubtedly was and is; and for that we praise him. We do not yet comprehend precisely all the workings of his ways; but we are convinced that though clouds and darkness are round about him, righteousness is the habitation of his throne.

A glorious purpose for the future of the human race has been revealed—a purpose, however, which has been crossed and checked, hindered and thwarted generation after generation. But God 'goes marching on' towards the final goal. Being resisted by the barriers of human greed, pride, infidelity or sensuality, he pleads, exhorts, warns and threatens; when all else has failed he destroys. As Anne of Austria said to Richelieu, 'God does not pay at the end of every day, my Lord Cardinal, but at the end he pays'. Only as a last resort does divine judgement begin to operate. Then our God is a Consuming Fire.

# Chapter 3

# ELISHA AND THE BEARS: THE PROPHET AND THE HOOLIGANS

Then it happened, as they continued on and talked, that suddenly a chariot of fire appeared with horses of fire, and separated the two of them; and Elijah went up by a whirlwind into heaven. And Elisha saw it, and he cried out, 'My father, my father, the chariot of Israel and its horsemen!' So he saw him no more. And he took hold of his own clothes and tore them into two pieces.

Then he went up from there to Bethel; and as he was going up the road, some youths came from the city and mocked him, and said to him, 'Go up, you baldhead! Go up, you baldhead!' So he turned around and looked at them, and pronounced a curse on them in the name of the Lord. And two female bears came out of the woods and mauled forty-two of the youths. (2 Kings 2:11–12; 23–24)

THIS Old Testament story is one which the sceptic and the critic seldom fail to hold up for our condemnation. It is referred to by the modernist as an indisputable proof

that in the records of the Old Testament there is much
that cannot be reconciled with a true conception of the
character of God. On the surface of the story there appears
to be room for that contention; and undoubtedly many
devout Christian believers have thereby become sorely
perplexed or mentally distressed. And, be it remembered,
the Bible does not pause to apologise or explain. Stumbling-
blocks to belief abound; they constitute a challenge to
sincere enquiry.

My attention was first drawn to the need for particularly
careful study of this incident by a remark made to me by
two brother clergy, both Cambridge honours men, before
whom I had submitted some weighty proofs from
archæological discovery of the historic integrity of the
Old Testament records. Compelled to admit the relevance
of much that was presented, they then pointed to this
story as a kind of black patch in the Scriptural revelation
which no archæological evidence could remove. This
attitude I found to be fairly common, and, in my experience,
one which has proved to be prejudicial to the content of
the written Word of God.

In an essay on the subject of 'The Bible and Its Value',
written by a former Canon of Westminster, in a volume
primarily designed for the edification of the Evangelical
clergy and laity of the Church of England, the author
writes: 'How, for instance, could the God of Love, the
Father, order the massacre of innocent Canaanite babes,
or send bears out of a wood to devour little children who
called Elisha "bald-head"?' Such records, he suggests,
can be summarily disposed of. 'We now feel ourselves,'
he says, 'free to reject as assertions of actual historical
fact some of the strange happenings in the Old Testament,

because they contradict what we know of God's method of operation.'[1]

The method of elimination is easy. Whatever in Holy Scripture does not square with our preconceived ideas may be obliterated. It is obvious, however, that such a method can have dangerous consequences. The penknife has been used in the past with disastrous results. But there is an alternative. Instead of drastic elimination, I suggest divine illumination. Elimination is easy: illumination costs. Its pursuit demands humility, study, and earnest supplication. Such requisites are particularly called for in the examination of difficult, challenging passages of Holy Scripture, particularly the one immediately before us.

I propose, therefore, that we examine this narrative with meticulous care to ascertain precisely what it contains and reveals. In doing so we shall only be following the oft-quoted counsel of Wycliffe, the great Bible scholar and reformer: 'It shall greatly help to understand Scripture if you mark not only what is spoken or written, but of whom and to whom, with what words, at what time, where, to what intent, with what circumstances, considering what goes before and what follows.'

In accordance with that precept, my aim is to study this brief Biblical narrative in the light of all its attendant circumstances. The enquiry can be conveniently pursued by dividing it under the following heads: (i) Who? (ii) Where? (iii) When? (iv) What? (v) Why? To be more precise, I suggest that we endeavour to answer, as fully as is possible, these questions, which are of fundamental importance: (i) Who were the persons concerned? (ii)

---

[1] VF Storr, *Liberal Evangelicalism*, pp. 84, 86.

Where did it occur? (iii) When exactly did it happen? (iv) What signified the cry and the curse? (v) Why should the record be rejected?

## (1) WHO WERE THE PERSONS CONCERNED?

This enquiry is of primary importance; for a serious misconception is widespread. The story has often been grossly misrepresented, somewhat after the following fashion. An old bald-headed prophet has attracted the attention of a group of innocent little children, playing in the main street of their home town. As he passes by, the children cry after him, more playfully than tauntingly, 'Go up, you bald head; go up, you bald head!' Immediately the old prophet, being very angry, turns round and curses them in the Name of the Lord. Forthwith, as a direct divine punishment, out from the adjoining wood rush two she-bears who 'devour' forty-two of the innocents. Such a description is a grotesque travesty of the entire proceeding.

Elisha, when the incident occurred, was certainly not an old man. Very probably he was not more than twenty-five years of age; for he lived for nearly sixty years after the date of this event.[1] Moreover, he was certainly not bald-headed, as will presently be demonstrated. Only a few years had elapsed since his ordination to the prophetic ministry. In the 19th chapter of 1 Kings we have a dramatic record of Elijah's journey to the home of Elisha, his divinely indicated successor, and what ensued. He finds the young man working on his father's farm, ploughing

---

[1] In the Chronological Appendix to Angus's *Bible Hand-Book,* Elijah's translation is dated 856BC; the death of Elisha, 797BC.

with the twelfth yoke of oxen. A simple but significant ceremony follows. Elijah, the old prophet, rapidly nearing the end of his ministry, casts his mantle over the shoulders of Elisha, who immediately discerns the import of the act. Ready immediately to obey the call, he yet manifests a tender, filial regard for his parents by running after Elijah and making the pathetic appeal, 'Please let me kiss my father and my mother, and then I will follow you'.

As to the character of Elisha, his life story reveals him as a gentleman in the truest sense of the word: merciful, beneficent, high principled, personally disinterested, while profoundly devoted to the service of Jehovah and the highest welfare of Israel. In his dignified personality and appearance he carried the evidence of his purity and consecration. Early in his ministry, while travelling on his missionary journeys, he attracted the attention of a woman of quality, the lady of Shunem, who, eager to provide hospitality for a faithful servant of the Lord, said to her husband: 'Look now, I know that this is a holy man of God, who passes by us regularly' (2 Kings 4:9).

The stormy ferocity of Elijah is wholly absent from the moral make-up of Elisha. The contrast between the two resembles the difference between the roaring of the wind and the lightning flash of the tempest which preceded, and the still small voice which followed, at the memorable theophany of Horeb (1 Kings 19:11–12).

Elisha's repugnance to anything savouring of vengeance is manifest in his dealings with the army of Syria, when it was miraculously blinded for a period and led helplessly into the heart of the city of Samaria. Having his enemy so completely in his grasp, the king of Israel cries out excitedly, 'My father, shall I kill them? Shall I kill them?'. Promptly comes the prophet's answer: 'You shall not kill them. Would you kill those whom you have taken captive with your sword and your bow? Set food and water before them, that they may eat and drink and go to their master?'. And the record proceeds, 'Then he prepared a great feast for them; and after they ate and drank, he sent them away and they went to their master'. This beautiful story of humanitarian clemency closes with the fitting sequel: 'So the bands of Syrian raiders came no more into the land of Israel' (2 Kings 6:21–23). It was a manifestation of the magnanimity of a great soul; it revealed the gentleness and nobility of character of the prophet. His recorded miracles prove to be for the most part gracious acts of beneficence and charity, provoked by tender sympathy with the needy and distressed.

Let us now turn to the other side of the picture in order to discover who precisely were the insolent assailants of the young prophet, as he journeyed along the main street of Bethel. It is an unfortunate translation of the Hebrew original that in the KJV they are described as 'little children'. Nearer to the truth is the rendering in the margin of the RV, 'young lads' (youths in the NKJV)

Now the Hebrew word which is translated 'children' in the KJV is *naarim,* the plural form of the word *naar,* which has a wide signification. According to the *Students' Hebrew Lexicon,* which has been my companion since college days, the word *naar* originally signified roughness; hence it came to mean youthfulness or youth, because of the roughness of speech of a boy who has attained the age of puberty. it was also employed to describe a servant or a soldier.

Two familiar instances of its use occur in the book of Genesis. In the story of the offering of Isaac on Mount Moriah, Abraham is arrested at the crucial moment by hearing the command spoken by the Angel of the Lord, 'Do not lay your hand on the lad (*naar*)' (Genesis 22:12). Isaac was then more than twenty years of age. Later, in the days of Jacob, it is recorded: 'Joseph, being seventeen years old, was feeding the flock with his brothers. And the lad (*naar*) was with the sons of Bilhah' (Genesis 37:2).

Centuries later, in the records of 2 Kings, the same word *naar* is employed to describe Gehazi as the servant of Elisha; and Gehazi at that time was obviously a young man who had attained maturity, or at least was near thereto. Close to the same period, in the days of Ahab the king, when a war of fierce destruction was threatened by Benhadad, the king of Syria, an unnamed prophet predicted that a victory for Israel would be achieved by a company of two hundred and thirty-two 'young leaders of the provinces' (1 Kings 20:14–15); and the Hebrew word translated 'young leaders' is *naarim*.

Therefore, to represent the assailants of Elisha at Bethel as a group of tiny children is not merely misleading; it is radically erroneous. In Ellicott's Commentary on the passage it is stated that the boys who mocked Elisha might be of various ages up to twenty. And the apt comment is added: '"Little children" would not be likely to hit upon a biting sarcasm, nor to sally forth in a body to insult the prophet.'

The Hebrew adjective *qatan* which occurs in its plural form *qetannim*, translated 'little' in the KJV, is frequently used to denote a younger son. This is seen in the following examples: 'She [Rebekah] sent and called Jacob her younger son' (Genesis 27:42), and 'There remains yet the youngest [David]' (1 Samuel 16:11). Neither Jacob nor David at the time referred to could have been described as little; moreover, David was there and then anointed to be king. Connecting the two Hebrew words together, Canon Rawlinson, in the exegetical section of *The Pulpit Commentary*, adopts the translation 'young lads', adding, 'boys, that is, from twelve to fifteen'. My own conviction is that our modern English 'young fellows' is the most accurate rendering of the original. But from their behaviour it is obvious that they belonged to the baser sort who might be described as hooligans.

We now perceive that what actually occurred differs vastly from the common misunderstanding of the event. Put in plain modern dress the incident might not unfitly be likened to a young inoffensive curate, recently appointed to a difficult and responsible city task, who, as he journeys in the direction of his mission district, is followed by a gang of street roughs or hooligans having no reverence for religion, ridiculing and reviling him solely because of his sacred vocation. It is not a pretty picture; even as it stands it stirs our indignation; but there is more to follow.

### (II) WHERE DID IT OCCUR?

The place was Bethel. The average reader passes over this detail without much consideration; but the place itself proves to be of paramount importance for a right understanding of the narrative.

When lecturing on the subject, I have occasionally asked the audience to do a bit of mental arithmetic. Here is the question: If two she-bears, emerging from a wood, attacked a crowd of youths so fiercely that forty-two of them were injured and some perhaps killed, how many were there in the crowd at the beginning? For one naturally assumes that the moment the she-bears appeared there ensued a swift scattering of the gang in various directions. Judging from present experience of what might happen to a similar crowd in a modern city thoroughfare, it would not be an exaggeration to suggest that two got away for every one that was hurt; so that the gang of hooligans who followed Elisha must have numbered at least one hundred at the beginning. The question which naturally follows is, Why were there so many? And the answer is— because it happened at Bethel.

Bethel was a centre of apostasy in Israel throughout many generations. It occupies a prominent place in the story of the rebellion of Jeroboam, the son of Nebat, during the reign of Rehoboam the son of Solomon, which is so graphically recorded in 1 Kings 12. Jeroboam created a split in the twelve tribes of Israel. He succeeded in breaking away from their allegiance to the throne of David the ten Northern tribes, leaving only to Rehoboam the two tribes of Judah and Benjamin. Then followed an astute manoeuvre. In order to make the severance sure and lasting, he decreed that the rebellious tribes should no longer go up to Jerusalem to worship. Instead, he caused to be made two calves of gold, one of which he placed in Dan in the extreme northern portion of his territory, and the other in Bethel, at the southernmost point, which was situated twelve miles north of Jerusalem. When this was accomplished he issued a proclamation to his subjects in the words: 'It is too much for you to go up to Jerusalem. Here are your gods, O Israel, which brought you up from the land of Egypt!'

Irregular ordination of priests, and flagrant abuses of the divine law followed. The usurper set apart priests out of the families of the common people indiscriminately;

including many who were in no way connected with the tribe of Levi; and it is stated that 'at Bethel he installed the priests of the high places which he had made' (1 Kings 12:32). There apparently a royal chapel was built (Amos 7:13); and then it is said that he himself assumed priestly functions, 'sacrificing to the calves that he had made'. The name of Jeroboam became thereafter a byword of infamy. Repeatedly in the Scriptural records occurs the national verdict of his condemnation, 'Jeroboam the son of Nebat, who had made Israel sin' (1 Kings 22:52; 2 Kings 3:3; 10:29; 13:2; 14:24; 15:9, 18, 24, 28; 23:15).

Turning to the writings of the contemporary prophets, Amos and Hosea, we discover a dark picture of Bethel as the centre of deepening apostasy from the pure worship of Jehovah, and a focus of the idolatrous rites of the nations round about. Severe prophetic denunciations abound. Amos utters a solemn warning in the words: '"Hear and testify against the house of Jacob," says the Lord God, the God of hosts, "that in the day I punish Israel for their transgressions, I will also visit destruction on the altars of Bethel; and the horns of the altar shall be cut off and fall to the ground' (Amos 3:13–14). Note the two-fold reference to 'the altars' and 'the altar'. The latter is apparently the altar of the golden calf set up by Jeroboam, while the former refers probably to the idolatrous cults which had gathered around the central profanity of the worship of Jehovah. A more terrifying warning from Amos follows: 'For thus says the Lord to the house of Israel: "Seek me and live; but do not seek Bethel, ... For ... Bethel shall come to nothing. Seek the Lord and live, lest he break out like fire in the house of Joseph, and devour it, with no one to quench it in Bethel' (Amos 5:4–6).

In the prophecy of Hosea (Hosea 4:15) the degeneration of Bethel, which had such sacred associations in the days of Jacob, is marked by a change of name to express its condemnation. Bethel, which means a House of God, becomes Beth-aven, the House of Vanity or Nothingness— a contemptuous reference to the idol divinities who could neither hear nor see. And the desolation of its impending judgement is vividly pictured in the words: 'Also the high places of Aven, the sin of Israel, shall be destroyed. The thorn and thistle shall grow on their altars; they shall say to the mountains, "Cover us!" and to the hills, "Fall on us!"' (Hosea 10:8).

What Rome was to the reformers Luther, Calvin, and John Knox, that Bethel came to be in the eyes of the faithful prophets of Jehovah—the focus of Israelitish idolatry. We can well imagine how bitter was the enmity between the fiercely zealous Elijah and the renegade Israelites who served at the altars of Bethel. And correspondingly we can perceive the reason for the immense concourse of irreverent youths who followed Elisha, his successor, as he passed along the main street of their city. Doubtless they were for the most part sons or near relations of the priests of the infamous idolatry which had provoked the fiery denunciation of the true servants of God. So, when Elisha, wearing Elijah's mantle, passed by, they hailed him and mocked him as the new champion of that pure worship of Jehovah which they and their fathers had so persistently desecrated and rejected. Hence the chorus of jeering and contemptuous reviling which proceeded so loudly from their lips.

## (III) WHEN EXACTLY DID IT HAPPEN?

Time can be of supreme importance. Upon the ascertainment of the precise hour of occurrence may depend the verdict which will condemn a man to death or set him free. In order to estimate the real significance of this Biblical record it is indispensably necessary to have clearly in mind the historic background—the events which immediately precede and which ultimately follow.

The chapter opens with a plain intimation of the date. It occurred within a period of five or six days following the majestic translation of Elijah into the heavens. It was a time of acute crisis in the history of Israel. Elijah, the fiery champion of Jehovah, jealous for the glory of his Lord, had become sorely distressed and disheartened because of the growing alienation of the people from the God of their fathers, and the worship which was due unto his holy Name. So dejected had he become that he longed to die.

At Horeb a reaction had set in, following the temporary triumph on Mount Carmel, when a battalion of the degraded priests and prophets of Baal and other heathen divinities had been overwhelmed by the heroic faith of this brave and mighty prophet of Jehovah. But even he quailed before the threats of the powerful, vindictive, ruthless Jezebel, through whose influence these various Phoenician cults had been introduced into Israel. In the wilderness of Beersheba, whither he had fled at first, he made earnest supplication that he might die. He was finished! 'It is enough!' he said; 'Now, Lord, take my life, for I am no better than my fathers!' (1 Kings 19:4). Forty days later, at Horeb, while sheltering in a cave in the mountains, he hears the still small voice of the Lord questioning him: 'What are you doing here, Elijah?' Note the answer of utter despair: 'I have been very zealous for the Lord God of hosts; because the children of Israel have forsaken your covenant, torn down your altars, and killed your prophets with the sword. I alone am left; and they seek to take my life' (1 Kings 19:13–14).

The religious condition of the nation was bad, yet not quite so bad as it appeared in the eyes of the prophet. Apparently the whole nation had apostatised; nevertheless there were known to God, though hidden from the sight of men, some seven thousand valiant and devoted Israelites who had kept the ancient faith, refusing to bow the knee to Baal. Jehovah has this faithful remnant still; yet what a feeble minority it is! Only seven thousand out of the hundreds of thousands of the elect people of God in Israel! It must appear strange to us to read that at such a crisis in the nation the prayer of Elijah was heard and answered. He had finished his course; his faithful ministry was nearing its end; and by the power of Jehovah he will presently be rewarded by a swift and glorious translation from earth to heaven. But not before his successor has been appointed and initiated. Accordingly, prominent in the divine instructions given to him, occurs the explicit command: 'And Elisha the son of Shaphat of Abel Meholah you shall anoint as prophet in your place' (1 Kings 19:16).

What a perilous position, what a grave responsibility for a young man to undertake! Well might Elisha have asked: Who can succeed where Elijah has failed? What man is sufficient for these things? The knowledge that Elijah is about to be taken away burdens his soul with fearful apprehension of impending disaster. How can we survive the loss of our national protector? What can I do, he says, when my master is gone and I am left alone?

When presently certain students belonging to one of the theological schools, which existed for the training of prophets and teachers of religion, approached him with the enquiry, 'Do you know that the Lord will take away your master from over you today?' they receive a curt answer, prompted by the bitterness of his soul. 'Yes,' he says, 'I know; keep silent!'

Finally, after the long journey down to Jericho is finished, and they are nearing the lonely Jordan locality where the separation is destined to take place, Elijah, solicitous for the welfare of his young successor, says, 'Ask! What may I do for you, before I am taken away from you?' What can Elisha ask save for that which shall relieve the burden on his heart: 'Please,' he answers, 'let a double portion of your spirit be upon me.'

They continue to walk and commune together until suddenly they are parted by some mysterious angelic intervention; and immediately the heart of Elisha begins to fail. When the old champion is swept away by the whirlwind, and gloriously exalted by the chariot of fire, a bitter cry of anguish is heard, expressing the feeling of desolation and weakness in the young man's heart: 'My father, my father, the chariot of Israel and its horsemen!' Like the retreat of a mighty army leaving a land utterly defenceless—so seemed this sudden, swift departure of Elijah in the eyes of Elisha, his inexperienced successor, left to carry on in the midst of an apostate nation going from bad to worse.

It is thus clearly manifest that this incident at Bethel occurred at one of the grave crises in the history of Israel, when God's truth and the highest interests of his elect people were seriously imperilled—a fact which is completely ignored by the average reader of the story.

## (IV) WHAT SIGNIFIED THE CRY AND THE CURSE?

We now reach the crucial problem of the narrative. After lingering for a few days in the Jericho district when, being solicited, he exercised a healing ministry, the young prophet prepares to return to his headquarters in Samaria. Bethel lies along the route. A distance of about twenty miles separated it from Jericho, necessitating a toilsome ascent. For Bethel is the highest northern point in the rocky backbone of Palestine which lies parallel to the Jordan valley. A long weary journey is before Elisha. To reach Bethel he has to ascend to a height equal to that of one of our highest mountains. Jericho lies some 1,300 feet below the level of the Mediterranean Sea, while Bethel was situated about 2,000 feet above. The brevity of the Scriptural narrative may easily mislead; certain significant details can easily be overlooked. We need to picture in imagination the grim reality—a hot, extremely fatiguing journey on foot, by a young prophet travelling through a hostile district, his heart filled with foreboding as to the future and the consciousness of his own inadequacy for the task set before him. In the meantime the news has travelled along the caravan route. It is reported that Elijah has mysteriously departed; but the students in the schools of the prophets have already recognised that the mantle of the master has fallen upon the disciple. 'The spirit of Elijah rests on Elisha.'

The news, which travelled fast in those days, has undoubtedly reached the inhabitants of Bethel. They had reason to be particularly interested. It is widely discussed; and the young men of Bethel prepare to give Elisha a welcome accordant with the carnality of their minds and the corruption of their hearts. We can imagine the scene. 'Come on, lads! Here is Elisha, the successor of Elijah.' The summons meets with a ready response. The crowd of young hooligans, perhaps incited by their idolatrous parents, soon grows, and as it grows it becomes more hostile and cruel. Following closely on the heels of the young prophet, walking alone, they create a noisy clamour, shouting loudly, 'Go up you bald head; go up you bald head!'

What precisely did the cry signify? It should be remembered that in translating from one language to another, a word may lose its entire significance. Here is a simple illustration. In my student days, to describe an undergraduate as a bounder, was to reach the limit of offensiveness. But if that word bounder were to be translated literally into French, it would signify to readers on the other side of the Channel that that undergraduate was an athlete! There are idiomatic expressions in English which simply cannot be rendered literally in another tongue without loss of meaning. This applies to some common terms of speech and certain abusive epithets, not unfamiliar in our police courts, which need not be particularised. I have it on high authority that this word belongs to such a category. There is a meaning in the Hebrew term, as originally employed, which is lost in our English version.

A medical man of my acquaintance, an Arab born in Egypt, who was decorated in the First World War, helped me to solve the problem. When I questioned him, he promptly assured me that in the East, even to this day, 'you son of a bald head', is one of the most offensive epithets which one person can hurl at another. The offensiveness of the term has originated in the fact that in the orient baldness has long been regarded as an incipient sign of leprosy.[1] Certain it is that when addressed to Elisha it was an expression of extreme contempt.

As to the real meaning of the cry, 'Go up!' there is little room for doubt. The opening words of the chapter literally translated from the Hebrew, read: 'When the Lord would cause to *go up* Elijah.' The verb rendered 'go up,' in the taunt addressed to Elisha, is precisely the same as that which occurs in this first verse. And the significance of the cry is not far to seek. It was a challenge to the young prophet to follow his master. It may be that those irreverent youths affected to disbelieve the report of Elijah's translation, and so issued their mocking challenge. Whether that be so, certain it is that their whole attitude was one of godless defiance and contemptuous rejection of this new prophet of Jehovah, whose worship they and their fathers had so ignominiously desecrated or destroyed.

'So he turned around and looked at them, and pronounced a curse on them in the name of the Lord.' What ensued is bluntly described in the brief record which follows: 'And two female bears came out of the woods and mauled forty-two of the youths.' Note the word 'mauled'. Whether any were killed, or how many of the original gang escaped, is not stated; but forty-two were at least badly mauled, if not seriously injured. Bethel then received a warning which undoubtedly created a profound impression. Contempt for God's faithful servants is always perilous. Is it not written: 'Do not touch my anointed ones, and do my prophets no harm'? God keeps the feet of his saints. But I am persuaded that the condemnation pronounced by the prophet was not provoked by a sense of personal insult. He was jealous

---

[1] *Vide* Leviticus 13:42–44.

for the honour of Jehovah; he recognised that it was not the servant of the Lord who was being ridiculed and reviled, but the Lord himself. And it was in the Name of that Lord whom they had rejected and despised that he pronounced the curse of condemnation. By some flash of divinely inspired intuition, such as Elisha manifested more than once in his later ministry, he appears to have foreseen the dread calamity which was impending. Whether the prophet's curse directly evoked the swift punishment which followed we cannot decide. It might be argued that the yells of a hundred excited hooligans would suffice to alarm the she-bears who were guarding their cubs in the dense forest which was in the neighbourhood. It is not always necessary for the Almighty God to intervene directly in the punishment of transgressors of his laws. Sin brings punishment in its train, as night follows day, and paves the way of ultimate calamity. But if God did not directly send, he assuredly permitted these fierce instruments to effect a judgement which was as terrifying as it was unexpected.

### (v) WHY SHOULD THE RECORD BE REJECTED?

Confessedly a problem is presented. Many suggest that in this narrative we have a judgement which offends the moral consciousness; and of course elimination provides an easy way out. But I personally am not prepared to tread that path. At least two grave reasons may be submitted for the retention of the story as an example of God's righteous dealings with mankind.

First, a signal judgement upon the wicked may be necessary as a means of protection of the pure and innocent. Here is an illustration which might be said to be drawn from life. The headmaster of one of our big public schools in England has intimated to their parents that two of his senior boys in the sixth form are about to be expelled. They have been proved guilty of acts of contamination; endeavouring to initiate junior boys into the secrets of abominable vice. The parents of the two seniors are seriously alarmed. They expostulate in the presence of the headmaster in terms such as these: 'You are going to blast the entire future of these two young men, just about to enter the University to prepare for a career of public service. They will carry the stain of their expulsion upon their character for ever. It will prove an insuperable obstacle to their advancement in any direction. Surely you are not going to carry into execution this terrible threat, condemning them to everlasting disgrace.'

But the headmaster is adamant; the decision is irrevocable. He replies in effect: 'I have no other course before me. I must do my duty. In this school there are six hundred boys. A plague of immorality may quickly spread if I do not take instant pains to check it. At all costs I must protect the innocent and the unwary.' Ultimately the expulsion takes place; and the whole school becomes aware of it. Was the action of that headmaster just or unjust? The answer is not in doubt. A thousand parents would applaud him for his high principle and moral courage. And shall not the judge of all the earth do right? Shall he not be just, especially in all that pertains to the protection of the loyal in act and the pure in heart?

Secondly, a signal judgement may sometimes be necessary as a warning lest worse befall. A loving mother will sometimes permit a disobedient child who persists in playing with fire to burn its hand. She does so because she dreads a more serious calamity. The renegade youths of Bethel, who so venomously assailed Elisha, were the direct ancestors of a generation which was swept into captivity because of its abominable sins in the sight of the Lord, notwithstanding the repeated admonitions of his prophets. Not much more than a century later, the threatened invasion of Israel by the armies of Assyria began; so that some of the grandchildren of the assailants of Elisha were numbered amongst those who suffered from the unspeakable horrors perpetrated upon all by the Huns of ancient days—then the most powerful military race in the world.

The grim record reads: 'In the ninth year of Hoshea [king of Israel], the king of Assyria [Tiglath Pileser] took Samaria and carried Israel away to Assyria, and placed them in Halah and by the Habor, the River of Gozan, and in the cities of the Medes. For so it was that the children of Israel had sinned against the Lord their God, who had brought them up out of the land of Egypt, from under the hand of Pharaoh king of Egypt; and they had feared other gods ... They set up for themselves sacred pillars and wooden images on every high hill and under every green tree. ... There they burned incense on all the high places ... and they did wicked things to provoke the Lord to anger, for they served idols, of which the Lord had said to them, "You shall not do this thing"' (2 Kings 17:6–12).

The dread calamity of transportation occurred in spite of the many exhortations and admonitions which were addressed to this favoured race, to bring them to a right mind and an obedient heart. But all in vain. For the record proceeds: 'Yet the Lord testified against Israel and against Judah, by all of his prophets, every seer, saying, "Turn from your evil ways, and keep my commandments and my statutes, according to all the law which I commanded your fathers" ... Nevertheless they would not hear, but stiffened their necks, like the necks of their fathers, who did not believe in the Lord their God' (2 Kings 17:13–14).

Could the contemptuous young hooligans of Bethel in the days of Elisha have had a vision of the future—the horrible torture and appalling destitution which would descend upon their posterity, as a direct consequence of persistent contempt for God's holy word and commandment—they would surely have hesitated before acting as they did.

The late Professor Sayce has described the revolting *modus operandi* of Assyrian invasion in vivid terms: 'The barbarities which followed the capture of a town would be almost incredible, were they not a subject of boast in the inscriptions which record them. Assurnatsir-pal's cruelties were especially revolting. Pyramids of human heads marked the path of the conqueror; boys and girls were burnt alive or reserved for a worse fate; men were impaled, flayed alive, blinded, or deprived of their hands and feet, of their ears and noses, while the women and children were carried into slavery, the captured city plundered and reduced to ashes, and the trees in its neighbourhood cut down. ... How deeply seated was the thirst for blood and vengeance on an enemy is exemplified in a bas-relief which represents Assur-bani-pal and his queen feasting in their garden while the head of the conquered Elamite king hangs from a tree above.'[1]

The tenderness in the heart of God is the outstanding theme of the book of Jonah. Nineveh, the world metropolis,

---

[1] *Assyria: Its Princes, Priests and People*, p. 127.

was a great city, but one which was exceedingly wicked. Its destruction was divinely decreed. But God's messenger was sent to proclaim a message of doom, which proved to be a message of mercy. For the citizens of Nineveh repented; all, from the king on the throne to the humblest of his subjects, clothed themselves in sackcloth and cried aloud in penitence; and the impending destruction of the Assyrian capital was postponed. God stayed his hand. He is not willing that any should perish. To that end he sends his prophetic messengers to give warning by word and deed. At Bethel one was startlingly presented. Had the sons and the fathers in Bethel taken to heart the lesson which they needed, and which was so alarmingly enacted before their eyes, the depopulation and devastation of Northern Israel might never have been, or might at least have been postponed.

But they and their successors persisted in flagrant disobedience; they continued to walk in their own ways; they worshipped according to the evil imaginations of their own hearts; they descended deep into a loathsome pit of greed and drunkenness, of gross idolatry and foul immorality, until they reached the limit. How pathetic is the summary statement which occurs in the closing chapter of the Books of Chronicles, depicting the patient but fruitless forbearance of Jehovah in his dealings with his chosen but rebellious people: 'And the Lord God of their fathers sent warnings to them by his messengers, rising up early and sending them, because he had compassion on his people and on his dwelling place. But they mocked the messengers of God, despised his words, and scoffed at his prophets, until the wrath of the Lord arose against his people, till there was no remedy' (2 Chronicles 36:15–16).

# Chapter 4

# ANANIAS AND SAPPHIRA: JUDGEMENT IN THE HOUSE OF GOD

But a certain man named Ananias, with Sapphira his wife, sold a possession. And he kept back part of the proceeds, his wife also being aware of it, and brought a certain part and laid it at the apostles' feet. But Peter said, 'Ananias, why has Satan filled your heart to lie to the Holy Spirit and keep back part of the price of the land for yourself? While it remained, was it not your own? And after it was sold, was it not in your own control? Why have you conceived this thing in your heart? You have not lied to men but to God. Then Ananias, hearing these words, fell down and breathed his last. So great fear came upon all those who heard these things. And the young men arose and wrapped him up, carried him out, and buried him. Now it was about three hours later when his wife came in, not knowing what had happened. And Peter answered her, 'Tell me whether you sold the land for so much?' She said, 'Yes, for so much.' Then Peter said to her, 'How is it that you have agreed together to test the Spirit of the Lord? Look, the feet of those who have buried your husband are at the door, and they will carry you out.' Then immediately she fell down at his feet and breathed her last. And the young men came in and found her dead, and carrying her out, buried her by her husband. So great fear came upon all the church and upon all who heard these things. (Acts 5:1–11).

COMPETENT scholars throughout the world are now agreed that Luke, the author of the third Gospel and the book of the *Acts of the Apostles*, stands in the very first rank of historians ancient and modern. His historic statements have been tested in the crucible of an extremely fiery furnace; and they have emerged scathless. Sir William Ramsay, the brilliant classical scholar to whose devoted labours as an archæologist in Asia Minor the Church owes an incalculable debt, writes: 'I set out to look for truth on the borderland where Greece and Asia meet, and found it here. You may press the words of Luke in a degree far beyond any other historians, and they stand the keenest scrutiny and the hardest treatment, provided always that the critic knows the subject and does not go beyond the limits of science and justice.'[1]

With that testimony as a preface, let me tell an almost incredible but true story. An assistant bishop in a southern diocese was addressing a body of clergy of whom I happened to be one. He would certainly not have laid claim to any particular gift in the realm of scholarship. There are few voices but many echoes. It was obvious that his remarks on that particular occasion belonged to the latter category. He was very severe in his references to the content of the Old Testament, dwelling especially upon the severity of

---

[1] *The Bearing of Recent Discovery on the Trustworthiness of the New Testament*, p. 89.

the judgements recorded therein. He then very solemnly exhorted the brethren who were present not to allow the young people of their parishes to read the writings of Moses and the prophets. To support his appeal he told this story, which I do not hesitate to describe as apocryphal. A little girl had been reading much of the Old Testament. Eventually she reached the New. Then apparently she made a startling discovery, saying to her mother, 'Oh mother, how God has improved!'

In the discussion which followed I asked the bishop the question: 'Do you accept the historic integrity of the *Acts of the Apostles?*' His answer was, 'Of course I must'. I knew that he must. Then I put before him the problem which is thereby presented. Having regard to the nature of the offence committed, Luke's record of the condemnation of Ananias and Sapphira exhibits a divine judgement which apparently is more drastic and severe than any contained in the entire realm of the Old Testament.

It is a sad story—an ugly blot on the fair landscape of the Christian Church in the days of its infancy. It is the record of a deed which becomes exceedingly foul when viewed in the light of all the attendant circumstances. Unfortunately it must be true. No historian, certainly not Luke, would have gone out of his way to invent it; the temptation would have been to omit it; the Christian community of the faithful would have been eager to forget it.

## (1) FIRST PERSECUTION: SECOND PENTECOST

This break in the apostolic harmony occurred at an early and critical period in the history of the primitive church.

It was directly associated with the first persecution to which the disciples of Christ were subjected after their Master's Ascension. Peter and John had been arrested, and after a brief imprisonment were brought before the High Priest and the other ecclesiastics of Jerusalem. A notable miracle had been wrought at the hands of the Apostles—the healing of a crippled man, lame from his birth, who was very familiar to all passers-by because he was to be seen daily begging for alms 'at the gate of the temple which was called Beautiful'; and his miraculous restoration had become widely known. The offence with which Peter and John were charged was that they had ascribed this miracle of healing to the power of the Name of Jesus Christ, who had been crucified, but who was now risen from the dead, ascended and glorified.

It is a token of the historic integrity of the narrative that the principal opposition to the Apostles is here traced to the Sadducees. They were the dominating clique in the priestly power reigning at that time in Jerusalem. As a Jewish sect they denied the existence of angels, the immortality of the soul, and the resurrection of the body. The doctrine of the resurrection was to them peculiarly distasteful; they had challenged Christ concerning it; and now they discover, to their anger and mortification, the followers of Christ proclaiming it as the proof positive of the Messiahship of the crucified Nazarene.

After careful deliberation the final decision of the ecclesiastical court, called the Sanhedrim, is reported in the words: 'For, indeed, that a notable miracle has been done through them is evident to all who dwell in Jerusalem, and we cannot deny it. But so that it spreads no further among the people, let us severely threaten them, that from now on they speak to no man in this name.' To this

charge the apostles could only respond that they had no
alternative. 'We cannot but speak the things which we
have seen and heard' (Acts 4:16–20). No further
punishment by the court was inflicted; the terror of an
uprising among the people deterred them; but after being
repeatedly threatened should they persist in proclaiming
the resurrection of Christ, the Apostles were set free.

Thus a serious impasse was created between the powerful
priestly party and the weak, uninfluential, socially inferior
leaders of the infant Church. A thick cloud of threatened
persecution lay overhead; a serious barrier had been
erected. The Jewish ecclesiastics who had plotted to kill
the Prince of Life would not hesitate to excommunicate
and destroy any of his followers who dared to resist their
will.

The alarming news quickly spread throughout the
Christian community; the Church was in peril of being
strangled at its birth; the seriousness of the situation
could not be exaggerated. What could they do? The
answer is contained in the record that when the rumbling
of the threatening was heard 'they raised their voice to
God with one accord'. As before Pentecost, so now they
were 'all with one accord in one place' for one supreme
purpose—to pray for power from on high. Their earnest,
united, sustained supplication is concentrated in the
moving petition: 'Now, Lord, look on their threats, and
grant to your servants that with all boldness they may
speak your word, by stretching out your hand to heal,
and that signs and wonders may be done through the
name of your holy Servant Jesus' (Acts 4:29–30).

It was a cry of 'No Surrender'; an example of strong,
splendid faith in the power of their exalted Lord. And
the answer came from heaven impressively and convincingly.

The place of assembly was shaken; many were reminded thereby of the rushing of the mighty wind at Pentecost. The urge to prayer created a surge of the Spirit. A kind of second Pentecost ensued, as described in the sacred text: 'And when they had prayed, the place where they were assembled together was shaken; and they were all filled with the Holy Spirit, and they spoke the word of God with boldness' (Acts 4:31).

## (II) CHRISTIAN COMMUNISM: ALL THINGS COMMON

The first fruit of the Holy Spirit's indwelling is love. A heavenly inspiration, both wide and deep, took possession of the hearts of the disciples. Love abounded—love to God, and love unlimited to all the brethren in Christ. The love thus shed abroad was so intense that a wave of selflessness spread over the new community; self-centred interests began to disappear; care for the welfare of the poorer brethren began to occupy a prominent place in the minds and hearts of all. For Luke proceeds to relate: 'Now the multitude of those who believed were of one heart and one soul; neither did anyone say that any of the things he possessed was his own, but they had all things in common' (Acts 4:32).

This spontaneous movement of holy enthusiasm and widespread charity soon had its practical manifestation. It became concrete. Certain of the brethren started to part with their possessions. The funds of the Church began to be augmented by a voluntary sale of lands and houses, the proceeds being laid at the feet of the apostles to be distributed according to the measure of the need of the poorer disciples individually. It was a piece of Christian Socialism which was purely voluntary, not obligatory, in no sense political, having as the ultimate source of its origin the holy wind from the heavenly hills— the Breath of the Life-giving Spirit of God.

In this movement Barnabas, who was afterwards the companion of Paul, took a prominent part. Apparently he was the son of a rich native of Cyprus, and stood possessed of a considerable property. This he promptly sold and presented the total proceeds to the apostles for distribution among the poor. The amount thus obtained was obviously very considerable; for that particular incident created such widespread comment and such fervent gratitude, especially on the part of the poorer brethren, that it was singled out by Luke for special notice.

Earthly Utopias, however well conceived, fail to materialise. The reason is not far to seek. The best laid schemes are apt to founder on the rock of human infirmity or iniquity. A definite prophecy of the Master, too often forgotten, is now seen to be fulfilled. The Christian society of regenerate souls is the product of good seed sown in the hearts of responsive listeners to the inspired Word of God. But when the seed has thus been sown, then is the moment for the Satanic enemy of God and man to get busy. Secretly, as in a night when men are asleep, he oversows; with the pernicious result that just when a promising crop begins to appear, it is found that tares have been sown among the wheat! So it comes to pass that in the midst of this fair picture of apostolic simplicity and generosity we reach again one of the 'buts' of the Bible which introduces a dark, dismal story of human defection and deceit.

## (III) PETER AND ANANIAS

'But a certain man named Ananias, with Sapphira his wife, sold a possession. And he kept back part of the proceeds, his wife also being aware of it, and brought a certain part and laid it at the apostles' feet.'

The example of Barnabas, together with the deep and wide approbation which his magnanimity had created, stirred up in them both a spirit of emulation. They too wished to become prominent in the Church; aiming to be high lights, conspicuous because of the generosity of their alms-giving. Like Diotrephes, to whom John refers in his third epistle, they loved to have a position of pre-eminence. So they selected a certain property among their possessions and sold it; but unlike Barnabas and the other donors, they plotted secretly to reserve for their own use a portion of the proceeds, while pretending that what they were contributing represented the full value of that which was sold. It should be carefully remembered that there was no sin in their reservation of a part of the price received; the sin consisted in the deceit which they practised, when they brought only a portion to the Church while pretending that it was the whole.

Peter, an anointed apostle, was gifted with a spiritual intuition, a kind of second sight which was manifested on certain occasions by the prophets of the Old Testament and the apostles of the New. A searchlight of penetrating power radiated in the soul of Ananias as he stood before Peter. He had come with his gift of money anticipating high commendation, instead, he met with a rebuke of severest denunciation. Peter reasoned with the guilty man while he condemned him. 'Ananias,' he said, 'why has Satan filled your heart to lie to the Holy Spirit and keep back part of the price of the land for yourself? While it remained, was it not your own? And after it was sold, was it not in your own control? Why have you conceived this thing in your heart? You have not lied to men but to God.'

A sort of swift paralytic stroke seized the guilty man. So terrified was he by the tempestuous words of Peter that he completely collapsed; his heart ceased to beat. 'Then Ananias,' we read, 'hearing these words, fell down, and breathed his last.' The punishment, be it noted, was not inflicted by Peter. He dared not act in such a grave matter on his own authority, but only as he was inspired and directed by the Holy Ghost. The death of Ananias was an act of God. He was slain by the sword of a divine judgement.

## (IV) PETER AND SAPPHIRA

Three hours have elapsed. The sombre picture now takes on a still darker hue. The disciples have reassembled at the hour of prayer; and Sapphira, the wife of Ananias, appears in their midst. She is full of questioning. 'Where is my husband? I expected him home about three hours ago. I wonder where he can be.' The only reply which Peter vouchsafes to give her is in the nature of a searching enquiry. 'Tell me,' he asks, 'whether you sold the land for so much?' mentioning the false figure of Ananias. 'Yes, Peter,' she promptly answers, 'that was the exact amount.'

It is thought that by making this enquiry Peter wished to give her space for reflection and an opportunity for repentance. But it was all in vain. She, like her husband, lied unblushingly. She lied loudly with her lips; he lied silently in the act. Then Peter said to her, 'How is it that you have agreed together to test the Spirit of the Lord? Look, the feet of those who have buried your husband are at the door, and they will carry you out.' She straightway collapsed and died. And at that moment the young men who had just returned from the interment of Ananias entered into the assembly of the awed congregation. They were commanded to return forthwith with a second burden. 'And the young men came in and found her dead, and carrying her out, buried her by her husband.'

### (v) FEAR WITHIN THE CHURCH AND WITHOUT

The sad story ends with a twofold description of the alarming effect which was made upon the disciples who were inside the fold of the Church, and upon all the outsiders who became cognisant of the dread visitation. 'So great fear came upon all the church and upon all who heard these things ... none of the rest dared join them.'

It was at the height of our Lord's earthly ministry, at the apex of his popularity, that the Master uttered a solemn warning. Luke records that 'when an innumerable multitude of people had gathered together, so that they trampled one another, he began to say to his disciples first of all, "Beware of the leaven of the Pharisees, which is hypocrisy. For there is nothing covered that will not be revealed, nor hidden that will not be known"' (Luke 12:1-2). The Greek word for hypocrite means literally an actor. Pretence or play-acting in the realm of religion is peculiarly offensive in the sight of God. Witness the twenty-third chapter of Matthew's Gospel, wherein is contained the most awful denunciation of hypocrisy to be found anywhere; and all proceeding from the lips of Jesus.

How quickly the ferment of this unholy leaven began to operate is evidenced by the lamentable career of Judas Iscariot, of Ananias and Sapphira. Should it be left unchecked it will leaven the whole lump and bring the Church into a condition of almost complete corruption. Centuries of Christian history provide the witness. Therefore the leaven must be extirpated without delay, whatever the cost. As though by a divine decree, the bodies of Ananias and Sapphira are laid across the threshold of the Church to be a perpetual obstacle in the path of any hypocrite, who for some profane purpose, might seek to enter within the sanctuary. God has no favourites whose iniquities he can lightly disregard or dismiss. Rather does spiritual privilege involve grave responsibility; as Amos the prophet reminds the elect race when he declares: 'Hear this word that the Lord has spoken against you, O children of Israel, ... You only have I known of all the families of the earth; therefore I will punish you for all your iniquities' (Amos 3:1–2).

Judgement begins in the house of God; but it does not end there. The innate consciousness of this sets up a barrier; it explains the significant words, 'Yet none of the rest dared join them'. In days when it is the fashion to speak scornfully of empty churches and depleted congregations, how seldom does one find any reference to the first fundamental reason for this deplorable alienation. It is the consciousness of some iniquity in the heart, or of moral uncleanness in a secret place; of doings that dare not face the light; of an unchecked lust for carnal pleasures of the moment not to be renounced, which restrains tens of thousands in a Gospel-illuminated land from making any approach towards membership of the Christian Church. Conscience, which makes cowards of us all, builds an almost insurmountable barrier. Like those who remained outside the apostolic community in the earliest days of the Church, these too, out of fear of the consequences, refuse to join. How sad is the pathetic enquiry of the Christ to the remnant of his dwindling disciples, when nearing the close of his earthly ministry, 'Do you also want to go away?'

Hypocrites! By this appellation so commonly applied to Christians within the Church, many try to find a refuge of excuse for their wilful rejection of the Christ, who has to say to them as he did to many in the days of his flesh, 'you are not willing to come to me that you may have life'—the life that is life indeed. Upon such persons a real divine judgement is already beginning to operate. 'And this is the condemnation,' said Christ, 'that the light has come into the world, and men loved darkness rather than light, because their deeds were evil' (John 3:19).

Hypocrisy is rampant today outside the pale of Christian society. For there is no hypocrisy more hypocritical than that of the man of the world who tries to cover over the foulness of his own immorality by perpetually pointing the finger of derision at the failures and inconsistencies of professed followers of Christ, who indeed are the first to confess their imperfection with sorrow and with shame. Yes, there are some hypocrites in the professing Church; the New Testament does not conceal the fact; it exposes the duplicity of two conspicuous members in the early community; but their number is infinitesimal in comparison with the uncounted mass of hypocrites who are without. But whether within or without none shall escape the searching light and consuming fire of that divine judgement to which we are all tending. '"Can anyone hide himself in secret places, so I shall not see him?" says the Lord; "Do I not fill heaven and earth?" says the Lord' (Jeremiah 23:24).

Secondly, in their compact of deceit Ananias and Sapphira were treading upon peculiarly holy ground. A mighty spiritual and social uplift had been experienced in the brotherhood by a heavenly inspiration of impressive character. The movement towards a pure humanitarianism which ensued—a splendid outburst of Christian charity—was the product of the special effusion of the Holy Spirit in Pentecostal power. Ananias and Sapphira were fully aware of all this. Yet, knowing it, they stooped to the lowest depths of duplicity, as though God himself could not see. Ananias, as one of the apostolic company, was privileged to become possessed of the Spirit-filled heart of a consecrated Christian. Instead, he surrendered himself to be a Satan-filled instrument to corrupt the divine and harmonious Christian congregation. Hence Peter's stern rebuke, 'Why has Satan filled your heart to lie to the Holy Spirit?' By his very act he had lied unto Peter; but to emphasise the foulness of the deed Peter adds, 'You have not [only] lied to men but to God.'

There is a peculiar sanctity attached to every sphere of operation of the Holy Spirit. That is immediately suggested, as we ponder the solemn warning uttered by our Lord: 'Anyone who speaks a word against the Son of Man, it will be forgiven him; but to him who blasphemes against the Holy Spirit, it will not be forgiven' (Luke 12:10). It is again suggested in the severe condemnation pronounced by Peter upon Simon Magus. He, like many a modern medium, played upon the abject superstitions of the people by means of his sorcery and dabbling in the occult. But presently he himself sought and obtained baptism. Then, marvelling at the effects produced by the bestowal of the Holy Spirit upon the converts to the Faith through the prayers and laying on of the hands of the apostles, he thought he saw an opportunity of enhancing his own power and prestige among the half heathen people of Samaria, who at one time followed him crying: 'This man is the great power of God.' He, therefore, approached Peter to try to do a deal, bringing a sum of money for the purpose. 'Give me this power also,' he said, 'that anyone on whom I lay my hands may receive the Holy Spirit.' But Peter, curtly rejecting the profane advance, cut him to the quick with the words, 'Your money perish with you, because you thought that the gift of God could be purchased with money! You have neither part nor portion in this matter, for your heart is not right in the sight of God' (Acts 8:18–21).

God is not to be mocked; the Holy Spirit is not to be tempted or trifled with. Dr AJ Gordon, that highly illuminated teacher and divine of the last century, in his book, *The Holy Spirit in Missions*, has related the following remarkable story in the experience of the Rev. Isaac D Colburn, who was for twenty years a missionary in Burma.

A company of native Christians in the district of Thongzai, British Burma, had assembled on the banks of a pool to witness the baptism of several disciples. The surrounding rocks and hills were covered with spectators, who had gathered from the neighbouring region. Near the water stood a father and his son, the first of whom had made himself conspicuous by a most bitter opposition to the Gospel, and by most strenuous efforts to dissuade his heathen neighbours from becoming Christians. As the native pastor was opening the services at the pool, this opponent broke in with the most blasphemous interruptions, mingled with all manner of obscene gestures and lascivious demonstrations. The preacher repeatedly remonstrated with him; but his words only stirred him to a more flagrant outburst of wickedness.

The father and son now stripped themselves of their clothing and plunged naked into the water; and as the pastor was about to baptise a disciple, the old opposer caricatured the ceremony, seizing his son by the heels, dipping him several times in the water, and pronouncing over him the baptismal formula, coupling the name of the Trinity with the most horrible blasphemies, so that the services were completely stopped.

Standing on the bank of the pool among the company of Christians was a native Karen evangelist by the name of SAU WAH. With stern and commanding bearing he now rose up and called for silence. Then, turning to the old man in the water, he said: 'O full of all subtlety and mischief, thou child of the devil, thou enemy of all righteousness, wilt thou not cease to pervert the right ways of the Lord?' Those Christians who witnessed the scene declare that, as he spoke, the Holy Spirit seemed to fall on the assembly, with awful power and impression. The disturbers, as though suddenly smitten with terror, fled from the water, and ran up the hillside. But before going many rods both fell prostrate to the earth. At the conclusion of the service the Christians lifted them up and bore them to the village. The father was found to be dead, and, though the son afterwards recovered consciousness, the stroke proved fatal, and within a few months he followed his father to the grave.[1]

Finally, in the light of the moral collapse of Ananias, we can trace the steps whereby pride leads to presumption,

---

[1] pp. 109–111.

and presumption issues in profanity. The sordid story provides a reminder which is urgently called for in this day and generation. Respectability with irreligion is a characteristic of the times. Sins committed through the instrument of the body, such as drunkenness and sexual immorality, may not perhaps be so unblushingly exhibited as in a former generation; but there are sins of the soul, such as that intellectual pride which manifests itself in cynical contempt for the sacred things of the Christian religion, which are far more perilous, and ultimately more devastatingly destructive. Wilful rejection of the light which radiates from God's Holy Word; a sneering attitude towards the sanctity of the one day in seven divinely set apart for worship and meditation upon the things unseen; an utter disregard of all endeavour to train up the children of men to become the children of God, with a readiness, sometimes almost Satanic, to put stumbling-blocks in their path—these are the sins which especially provoke the wrath of God, because they set him at defiance.

It is in highly privileged lands like England and Scotland, where the holy Gospel can be freely preached without political interference, where churches abound through the munificence of supporters in the past, where the means of grace are to be had at the corner of every main street—it is in such an environment that cynical religious indifference and thinly-veiled contempt appear to flourish and the trumpets of infidelity may blare with impunity.

There are publicists in our midst today, notably among playwrights and novelists, who profit financially by parading their presumed intellectual superiority to every religious convention, because they choose to reside in the midst of a nominally Christian community. If they lived surrounded by an openly atheistic population their wares would not meet with such a ready sale. And they know it—which is one reason why they are content to remain in a community the moral and spiritual foundations of which they are out to destroy. In the realm of fiction it is recognised that limits are transgressed with brazen effrontery, and an untold number of innocent or unwary readers are thereby grossly deceived and some hopelessly corrupted.

But God is not lightly mocked. His patience seems to be inexhaustible, but it has its limits. At a later date, Luke relates a striking instance of the peril which attaches to spiritual arrogance and presumption.

During a period when the missionary activities of the Church were increasing on every hand, Herod Agrippa, a grandson of Herod the Great, the baby-killer, 'stretched out his hand to harass some from the church'. Among these James, the brother of the Apostle John, was executed by his orders. Out for popularity, he quickly perceived that such extreme persecution of the Christians was particularly gratifying to the unbelieving Jews. Thereupon he took the necessary steps to have Peter arrested, with the intention of dealing with him as a certain kinsman of his had disposed of John the Baptist. But Peter was miraculously rescued from imprisonment by an angelic intervention, the vivid portrayal of which suggests the recital of an eye-witness. Note particularly the knocking of Peter at the door of the house of Mary the mother of Mark, and the reaction of Rhoda, the housemaid, thereto. No fancy picture that (Acts 12:1–16)!

And now for the sequel. Herod Agrippa, greatly perturbed, has left Jerusalem and gone to Cæsarea. Discord, for some reason unknown, has arisen between him and the people of Tyre and Sidon. They, however, sought an armistice, desirous that cordial relations should be established, depending as they did upon Herod for their wheat supply; their country, as Luke records, was 'supplied with food by the king's country'. They therefore waited upon, and were obviously prepared to flatter him.

Herod, doubtless conscious of all this, made great preparation for the audience. Luke relates that upon a set day he arrayed himself in royal apparel and sat upon his throne, and, with this background of august pomposity, he made an oration unto them. 'The voice of a god and not of a man!' shouted the crowd of sycophantic suppliants who composed his audience. And the blasphemous cry gratified the proud, pompous king. But ere the echoes of the tumult had died away, Herod himself was inwardly stricken, and died suddenly and mysteriously; for an angel of the Lord smote him 'because he did not give glory to God' (Acts 12:20–23).

Luke, the cultured doctor of medicine and precise historian, who was naturally interested in such a remarkable case, describes the cause of death in brief but pregnant terms: 'he was eaten by worms'. Josephus, the contemporary non-Christian historian, who confirms the historicity of the narrative, says: 'Agrippa put on a garment made wholly of silver, and of a contexture truly wonderful, and came into the theatre early in the morning; at which time the silver of his garment being illuminated by the fresh reflection of the sun's rays upon it, shone out after a surprising manner, and was so resplendent as to spread an horror over those that looked intently upon him; and presently his flatterers cried out, one from one place, and another from another (though not for his good), that he was a god; and they added, "Be merciful to us;

for although we have hitherto reverenced you only as a man yet we shall henceforth acknowledge you as superior to mortal nature". Upon this the king did neither rebuke them nor reject their impious flattery.'[1]

Such profane folly was not confined to ancient times. Today in modern civilised lands man is deified and God is dethroned! That this spirit is now so flagrantly manifested in Germany should be a warning to us to guard against the beginnings of pride and arrogance, remembering always the subtle temptation in Eden, 'You will be like God'. For disaster waits in its train. The peril of the pride which issues in presumption and profanity lies in sometimes swift, but always certain, destruction from the presence of the Lord and the protection of his Almighty power.

---

[1] *Antiquities*, xix:8.

# Chapter 5

# DIVES AND LAZARUS: RICH INFIDEL AND GODLY PAUPER

There was a certain rich man who was clothed in purple and fine linen and fared sumptuously every day. But there was a certain beggar named Lazarus, full of sores, who was laid at his gate, desiring to be fed with the crumbs which fell from the rich man's table. Moreover the dogs came and licked his sores. So it was that the beggar died, and was carried by the angels to Abraham's bosom. The rich man also died and was buried. And being in torments in Hades, he lifted up his eyes and saw Abraham afar off, and Lazarus in his bosom. Then he cried and said, 'Father Abraham, have mercy on me, and send Lazarus that he may dip the tip of his finger in water and cool my tongue; for I am tormented in this flame.' But Abraham said, 'Son, remember that in your lifetime you received your good things, and likewise Lazarus evil things; but now he is comforted and you are tormented. And besides all this, between us and you there is a great gulf fixed, so that those who want to pass from here to you cannot, nor can those from there pass to us.' Then he said, 'I beg you therefore, father, that you would send him to my father's house, for I have five brothers, that he may testify to them, lest they also come to this place of torment.' Abraham said to him, 'They have Moses and the prophets; let them hear them.' And he said, 'No, father Abraham; but if one goes to them from the dead, they will repent.' But he said to him, 'If they do not hear Moses and the prophets, neither will they be persuaded though one rise from the dead.' (Luke 16:19–31).

HELL is taboo in modern theology. The doom of the ungodly lies outside the sphere of popular preaching today. The parable of the Prodigal Son, featuring the infinite love of the Eternal Father—that is a theme upon which all delight to expatiate. But the story of Dives and Lazarus, with the lurid picture of torment which it presents, is not palatable to modern taste, and therefore is best avoided!

No man ever spoke such wonderful words of love and sympathy, of tenderness and compassion, as the Man of Nazareth. Yet it is equally true that no man has ever uttered more terrifying words of warning to the hypocrite, the sensualist, the blasphemer and the blatant unbeliever. There is both sunlight and shadow in the divine revelation. This is especially manifest in that picture of contrasts which is commonly designated the Parable of the Rich Man and Lazarus. For Christ's graphic delineation is nowhere called a parable; it may be indeed just a picture drawn from life—a vivid description of what was actually perceived by the Son of God who had power of insight to penetrate the heart of man, and power of vision to pierce the veil which divides the seen from the unseen.

This marvellous story, which occurs nowhere else in the New Testament, falls naturally into three divisions: (i) The contrast in life; (ii) The contrast in death; (iii) The contrast in the world to come.

## (1) THE CONTRAST IN LIFE

'There was a certain rich man who was clothed in purple and fine linen and fared sumptuously every day. But there was a certain beggar named Lazarus, full of sores, who was laid at his gate, desiring to be fed with the crumbs which fell from the rich man's table. Moreover the dogs came and licked his sores.' Attention is first drawn to the magnificence of the rich man's dress—an upper woollen garment of Tyrian purple, and a tunic of fine white linen of Egypt—such as was worn only by kings, princes and nobles; and then to the luxuriousness of his living—a rich banquet daily, with a superabundance of wines and dainties.

In sharp contrast, Jesus pictures a helpless mendicant who was 'laid' (the Greek word literally means 'cast down') at the porch of the palatial mansion to receive perchance some of the fragments of the daily feast. Only once in our Lord's parables is a personal name mentioned. It is here. Lazarus, the current Greek form of Eleazar, comes from El-ezer, which means God helps. Why does Jesus mention the name if not to indicate the character of him who bore it? Lazarus evidently belonged to the class of the pious indigent—poor people whose confidence was in God. The name of the rich man is not given, because, as Augustine suggests, it was a name not found in the Book of Life. The beggar's pitiable condition, moreover, is accentuated by the description that his all but naked body is completely ulcerated, and his strength so feeble that he cannot drive away the fierce scavenger dogs, which roam the streets of Eastern cities, who approach him with tongues outstretched to lick his sores.

## (ii) THE CONTRAST IN DEATH

What a tremendous change ensues at the moment of death! Yet it is all vividly described in a single verse. 'So it was that the beggar died, and was carried by the angels to Abraham's bosom. The rich man also died and was buried.' There is no reference to the burial of Lazarus. A funeral, perhaps, was not possible. His ulcerated body may have been just torn to pieces by the scavenger dogs who were never far away. But though there was no procession of mourners to lament his departure, there was a convoy of angels specially commissioned to carry his soul into Paradise.

'The rich man also died and was buried.' Prominence is given to the record of his obsequies, which doubtless were magnificent and imposing. No money was spared to give his body a gorgeous funeral. All his relations were there; a long procession of distinguished citizens followed behind; the Death March was impressively played; a regiment of hired wailing women provided the unending chorus of lamentation; and the corpse was finally laid in a costly rock-hewn sepulchre, swathed in linen cloths with spices in rich profusion. 'He was buried'! The rich man's dead body had all that a dead body could have. But his soul passed on friendless, destitute, solitary, alone.

There were no guardian angels in attendance to carry his soul into the realm of the unseen.

## (III) THE CONTRAST IN THE WORLD TO COME

'And being in torments in Hades, he lifted up his eyes and saw Abraham afar off, and Lazarus in his bosom. Then he cried and said, "Father Abraham, have mercy on me, and send Lazarus that he may dip the tip of his finger in water and cool my tongue; for I am tormented in this flame".' Our English word Hell has a double meaning. Because of that unfortunate fact, confusion occasionally arises in the interpretation of Scripture. The word Hell occurs both in the Old Testament and the New as the equivalent of the Greek word *Hades*, or the Hebrew word *Sheol*, and means simply the underworld—the place of the departed, to which the souls of all men, the saved and the unsaved, go at the moment of death. But the word is found also in the New Testament as the equivalent of the Hebrew word *Gehenna*, which geographically was the place of burning outside the walls of Jerusalem to which the refuse of the town was taken to be destroyed.

Now the word Hell in the passage before us is the equivalent of Hades, as the Revised Version indicates. It means simply the abode of the dead, as distinguished from the land of the living. It is that realm of the unseen which is described when we recite in the Apostles' Creed, 'He descended into hell'. But, and this is a very impressive revelation, Christ teaches that Hades is divided into two distinct spheres or departments, and that a swift separation ensues immediately at the point of death. Lazarus goes into one which is called Abraham's bosom—a paradise of felicity; the rich man goes into the other—a place of torment.

In the hallowed description of the Lord's Supper it is particularly recorded that John occupied a place of honour. 'There was leaning on Jesus' bosom one of his disciples, whom Jesus loved' (John 13:23). Correspondingly 'Abraham's bosom' was a familiar figure among the Jews to describe an abode of heavenly felicity; it was the place to which Jesus pointed when he said to the penitent thief crucified by his side on Calvary, 'Today you will be with me in Paradise'. Among the Hebrews the faithful looked forward to be gathered like children into the security of the arms of their great father Abraham. And this, on the authority of Jesus the Great Teacher, became the happy heavenly abode of the poor pious beggar who used to lie for hours each day at the gate of the rich man's house, hoping to receive some scraps of food from his table.

## (IV) THE GREAT GULF FIXED

To the cry of the rich man in his anguish the answer of Abraham is cutting and terrifying: 'Son, remember!' In those two words there is intimated a close connection, an unbroken continuity of this life with the next. The permanence of memory is guaranteed. Without the continuance of memory we should lack the consciousness of our own personality; like some shell-shocked men in the war, rendered pitiable in the extreme, not knowing either their own name or their home or their previous occupation. Lost identity is the penalty of loss of memory.

But we are here assured that memory will continue in the future state. There is reason to believe that after death it will be intensified, so that things which we now seem to have forgotten will be restored, and made clear and distinct. Oliver Wendell Holmes, who was nearly drowned when a boy, says that 'all at once my whole past life seemed to flash before me as a train going a thousand miles an hour, if such a speed were possible, would pass in one long streak before the eyes of a person standing by the railroad'. When an object is photographed the picture at first is extremely faint, but after the film has been passed through the developing solution its outline becomes sharp and clear. It may be that our experience at the point of death will correspond and our memory be quickened and expanded. 'Son, remember'!

To the appeal of the sufferer for some alleviation of his torment Abraham replies in effect: Yours is an impossible demand. No one can pass from this sphere to the one in which you now dwell. For there is a great gulf fixed between the two, which is impassable. It is not possible for Lazarus to go to you as you desire. Neither is communication possible between this realm and the land of the living. It is therefore not possible for Lazarus to go to the home of your five brothers to warn them of the fate which awaits the godless and impenitent. Besides, they have Moses and the Prophets. If they truly desire light and guidance let them hear them, giving heed to their inspired words.

## (v) RETROSPECT, REMORSE, RETRIBUTION

In this very illuminating revelation, which might aptly be designated the parable of the rich infidel and the godly pauper, we have a divine judgement pronounced as it were by anticipation. It is a shadow cast before, projected into the arena of that future life to which we are all inevitably proceeding. It is a grave yet glorious reality which is presented in two contrasted panels by the Son of Man, who was the Son of God incarnate, the Light of the World. No other has ever appeared upon earth comparable to him as a source of illumination concerning the conditions of life beyond the grave.

At this point we need to remember a characteristic difference between the Old Testament and the New, namely, that the judgements recorded in the former relate, in the main, to groups, nations, and peoples; whereas in the latter they are concerned almost exclusively with individuals. This is of course a broad generalisation. Nevertheless the distinction holds. Dr JB Mozley, a former Regius Professor of Divinity in the University of Oxford, has written: 'When we examine the ancient mind all the world over, one very remarkable want is apparent in it, viz., a true idea of the individuality of man; an adequate conception of him as an independent person, a substantial being in himself, whose life and existence was his own. ... Oriental civil law formally recognised the judicial principle of extending the parent's guilt and punishment to the children, which it could have done only under a defective idea of the child's individuality, treating the child as a mere appendage of the father.'[1]

This principle is apparent in many of the Old Testament records of divine judgement. But in the days of Ezekiel we discover that a narrowing-down process has begun to operate, and the sense of individual responsibility now tends to become paramount. This is how the prophet

---

[1] *Ruling Ideas in Early Ages*, pp. 37–38.

reasons with God's elect people: '"What do you mean when you use this proverb concerning the land of Israel, saying: 'The fathers have eaten sour grapes, and the children's teeth are set on edge'? As I live," says the Lord God, "you shall no longer use this proverb in Israel. Behold, all souls are mine; the soul of the father as well as the soul of the son is mine; the soul who sins shall die"' (Ezekiel 18:2–4).

In this Christian dispensation it is manifest that the judgements of God apply to the lives of men and women individually. Paul, in his *Epistle to the Romans*, refers to a 'day of wrath and revelation of the righteous judgement of God, who "will render to each one according to his deeds": ... tribulation and anguish, on every soul of man who does evil, ... but glory, honour, and peace to everyone who works what is good, ... For there is no partiality with God' (Romans 2:5–11).

Individual responsibility is the characteristic note of the New Testament revelation. We are not going to be saved in groups. Nationality will not count; family relationships will bestow no title; to be the descendants of Abraham, or to be born into the citizenship of the British Empire, will guarantee no kind of favour or priority. The only thing that matters now and that will count hereafter is vital union with Christ in God, issuing in a character conformable to his will, manifested in love to him and in charity to our fellow-men. So, to the professed members of the Christian Church in Corinth, Paul writes: 'For we must all appear before the judgement seat of Christ, that each one may receive the things done in the body, according to what he has done, whether good or bad' (2 Corinthians 5:10).

Having the consciousness of our individual responsibility
clearly in mind, we may now conclude our survey of this
parable of future judgement by carefully considering
four points of paramount importance.

First, although inequality and injustice are patently
manifest here and now, it is clearly revealed that
readjustment and retribution will be perfect and complete
in the hereafter. Nothing is easier than to point the finger
of condemnation at the unhappy conditions of life which
exist; at the deplorable cruelties and inconsistencies
which abound. They baffle the efforts of the most earnest
reformers who aim at their removal. For evil is widespread
and deep-seated; the human heart is everywhere tainted
with depravity; sin manifests itself universally in selfishness
and sensuality. And prejudice against religion is easily
propagated. Far too long has the transforming power of
the Christian Faith been obstructed by the atheistic plea
that religion is only so much dope to keep the labouring
masses of the community quietly content under a grasping
dominion of capitalism. Quite recently, however, a big
confession has been made by a modern writer of practical
experience in labour movements.

> Expectation of life after death, said the secular reformer,
> led the masses to tolerate their appalling conditions because
> of their hope of heaven. Well! The secular reformer and
> the Marxian Socialist have had their will with a vengeance.
> The proletarian masses in every advanced capitalist country
> do not look to a heaven beyond death at all. They dismiss
> it with the utmost cynicism and contempt. 'Religion is the
> opium of the people?' ... They have rejected 'pie in the
> sky'. What do they get instead? Promises of pie in a Utopian
> future. ... As a life-long Socialist, even I am convinced that
> the rejection of the hope of heaven by the masses has not
> improved their prospect of a heaven upon earth. *On the*

*contrary, it has worsened it.* ... Consider what was once the most highly organised and advanced proletariat in Europe, and the most atheistic—the German. Has their rejection of heaven and their consequent concentration on immediate concrete reforms resulted in improvement?[1]

We can now recognise how needful and opportune is the teaching of our Lord concerning the relation of this life to the next. The pains and penalties, the honours and rewards of the judgements recorded in the Old Testament, were confined to the life which now is—the life in the body. But we live in the dispensation in which eternal life and immortality have been brought to light through the Gospel; and accordingly, the judgements of the New Testament are not restricted to life on earth, where there is 'no abiding', but are projected into the life of the world to come. Christ has shown us most vividly that readjustment and retribution will one day be realised in perfection— but not here. What could be clearer than the words of reminder and reproof which he puts into the mouth of Abraham in response to the rich man's poignant appeal: 'Son, remember that in your lifetime you received your good things, and likewise Lazarus evil things; but now he is comforted and you are tormented' (Luke 16:25).

Second, it is revealed that character here determines our destiny hereafter. Every man will go to his own place; and that place will be determined by the character of the soul which passes out from the seen into the unseen. Separation is an essential feature in judgement. What is seldom realised, however, is that a separation is even now proceeding in earthly relationships. A gulf is already beginning to be fixed. Character in the present determines

---

[1] DR Davies, *On to Orthodoxy*, pp. 142–143.

the nature of our companionships according to the old proverb that 'birds of a feather flock together'.

For we are fearfully and wonderfully made. There appears to be in each of us a recording instrument, working automatically within the innermost chamber of the soul. Every thought we cherish, every word we speak, every pure aspiration or ignoble desire we conceive and cultivate—all these are permanently recorded, being impressed upon the sensitive tablets of the heart. And just as there is a recording instrument working within, there is a revealing process continually in operation without; so that what we are in the depths of our being tends sooner or later to become manifest in our outward form. The bloated face of the drunkard, the petrified face of the miser, the brazen face of the harlot, are but gross examples of a law which is operating in every human life; so that to a careful observer, the glance of the eye, the shape of the mouth, the set of the features, the bearing of the body, the gait and manner of the movement—all tend to indicate the character and disposition of the individual. The body is sometimes described as the clothing of the soul. But we are so wonderfully made that the soul has apparently the power to cut out of the cloth a pattern which corresponds to its own innermost character. For, according to Spenser,

> Of soul the body form doth take,
> For soul is form and doth the body make.

Someone has said that when a man has passed the age of forty he may, by looking at his face in a mirror, anticipate the Day of Judgement. It is perhaps an extreme statement; but it contains a suggestion of truth which all would do well to ponder. Undoubtedly, indications of the character of our own individual immortality may now be detected.

The saints in Christ are beginning upon earth to be clad in their robes of white; while sensual men, whose supreme aim is to gratify their fleshly lusts, begin now to assume in their countenance that swinish aspect which betokens the degraded character of the soul within.

A pure and chaste woman in a railway compartment begins to feel uneasy as she looks at a man sitting opposite. He is a perfect stranger. She knows absolutely nothing about him. But she instinctively recoils from the nearness of his presence. In her heart she knows that she could never trust him. His character is too clearly manifest in his face. Presently she goes out of the compartment, seeking a seat elsewhere.

Thus even on earth our character determines the quality of our companionship. Can two walk together except they be agreed? How many upright God-fearing citizens there are in our midst who, looking back, can trace with bitter sorrow an ever widening breach which separates them from the closest companions of their youth. What is experienced here in part is a foretaste of what will be experienced in perfection hereafter. No real fellowship is possible between truly consecrated Christians and utter worldlings and wantons who live without God, intent only upon the pleasures and pastimes of time and sense. A gulf is already being fixed which is destined hereafter to become a yawning chasm, and one that can never be bridged. Said the Master: 'Those who want to pass from here to you cannot, nor can those from there pass to us.'

Should the question be asked: If the gulf between the souls in the Paradise of felicity and those in the place of anguish be so vast and so impassable, how was it possible for the rich sensualist in his misery to see Lazarus and to speak to Abraham? An answer may be found in the suggestion that the realities of the world unseen transcend all the powers of our imagination. We do know, however, that communication actually exists today which our forefathers would have deemed miraculous or utterly impossible. The mysteries of wireless telephony and television are portents and prophecies of greater mysteries yet to be revealed. Distance, as we reckon it, is destined to be annihilated; but the chasm which separates in the realm of character will remain. What a solemn, terrifying note of finality is contained in that judgement which is pronounced in the last chapter of the last book of the Bible: 'He who is unjust, let him be unjust still; he who is filthy, let him be filthy still; he who is righteous, let him be righteous still; he who is holy, let him be holy still' (Revelation 22:11).

Third, the hellish agony of the lost is portrayed in a manner which is as terrifying as it is unmistakable. Burning flame and torment, unsupportable thirst and water longed for to cool the tongue—these of course are figures, but they are figures which represent realities. The sense of things unseen can only be conveyed to our understanding by means of the things that are seen—the things we actually know. These words, which proceeded from the lips of Jesus Christ, surely suffice to convey to our minds some conception of the indescribable horrors which await the sensually impenitent, the godlessly selfish and the cynically unbelieving.

'Hell is a philosophical necessity.' Human nature being what it is, and the products of sin and sensuality being what they are, it might reasonably be argued that if there is no hell there cannot be a heaven. Protestantism and Catholicism unite to emphasise the certainty of the doom of the ungodly and impenitent. The late Monsignor Hugh

Benson has said, from the Roman Catholic standpoint: 'To deny the possibility of an eternal exclusion from God's presence is to deny implicitly the reality of man's freewill. If everyone is to go to heaven finally, whether they choose it or not, then life is only a kind of game and men mere pawns that are all put back into the box at the end.' Correspondingly, Dr FB Meyer, a representative divine of the Free Churches, has said: 'It is impossible to accept the teaching of Jesus Christ as the authoritative and final word of God without believing that there is certainly a hell as there is a heaven.'

In Mark 9:43–44, our Lord uttered one of the most solemn warnings that ever proceeded from his lips: 'If your hand causes you to sin, cut it off. It is better for you to enter into life maimed, rather than having two hands, to go to hell *(Gehenna)*, into the fire that shall never be quenched where "Their worm does not die, and the fire is not quenched".'

It is unfortunate that the English word hell has two distinct meanings. This I have already briefly indicated; but for the sake of clarity I will risk repetition. It is found as the equivalent of the Hebrew *Sheol* and the Greek *Hades*, which denote merely the underworld or the place of the dead irrespective of character. But in the passage before us the word hell is the English translation of the Hebrew *Gehenna*, and signifies a place of fiery destruction. In the days of our Lord, Gehenna was a geographical locality in the valley of Hinnom on the west side of Jerusalem. In that valley fires were kept burning perpetually. Thither the rubbish and refuse which might pollute and poison the atmosphere were conveyed in order to be destroyed. Thus Gehenna was Jerusalem's well-known city destructor, where the fires burned without ceasing.

No warning, therefore, could be clearer than that contained in Christ's awful words. It is as though the Master said, 'Cut off your hand, cut off your foot, pluck out your eye, sacrifice your most precious possession should it prove to be a stumbling-block in the way of the life eternal, rather than run the risk of losing your all in the unquenchable fire of everlasting destruction from the presence of the Lord'.

I submit, however, that we have no sure warrant for building upon this figurative language of our Lord the doctrine of the total and final annihilation of the wicked. 'Without a parable he did not speak to them.' That was the Master's method. Each parable has its own special point of application. To enforce every detail is to miss the heart of the message in the main. Christ's injunction 'to turn the other cheek', for example, provides no warrant for perpetual pacifism. It should suffice, therefore, to emphasise that the picture of Jerusalem's city destructor, as exhibited by our Lord, provides a most solemn warning of the ultimate fate of the openly godless and avowedly profane—a fate which, I believe, in the degree of its irreparable loss and unspeakable pain—and that eternal—transcends the power of the human imagination to conceive.

Finally, the cause of the damnation of Dives is clearly revealed. It was not his wealth that destroyed him, but his infidelity and inhumanity. The superficial reader of the Scripture may easily jump to the conclusion that the pampered epicure perished because of his former opulence, while the famished mendicant was graciously rewarded because of his previous poverty. Such an interpretation is of course entirely false. God does not condemn any man because of his business success and consequent prosperity: 'Do you see a man who excels in his work? He will stand before kings.' Wealth, according to Old Testament standards, was regarded rather as a mark of divine favour.

It was not then the rich man's wealth, but his rank infidelity, manifested in his inhumanity, which was the cause of his downfall. His inhumanity shows itself in his utter disregard of the commandments of God concerning our attitude towards our fellow-men. 'You shall love the Lord your God with all your heart … And … you shall love your neighbour as yourself.' Lazarus, the helpless beggar, was a very near neighbour, lying hungry, ulcerated in body, and utterly destitute at the rich man's gate. And there were no doles, no hospitals, no poor relief institutions, in ancient days. But the rich sensualist, though knowing all this, bestowed not a single thought upon his neighbour's need. Why? Because self was the only god he worshipped, and self-indulgence the only aim and aspiration in life to which he gave earnest heed. Lazarus had for a name, God is my Helper: the rich man was nameless; his name had no place in the Book of Life, because he himself had no use for God and the riches of his grace.

His infidelity is revealed again in the piteous appeal which he makes to Abraham: 'I beg you father, that you would send Lazarus to my father's house, for I have five brothers who are infidels like I used to be, that he may testify to them lest they (also) come into this place of torment.' Now he can realise the peril which lies in their path. Someone, he thinks, should go to them immediately, and give them a warning which they cannot possibly ignore. How significant is the answer which Christ puts into the mouth of Abraham: 'They have Moses and the

Prophets in the inspired Scriptures, as a guide of life. Let them hear and take counsel from them.'

'Yes,' replies the rich man, 'I know all that; but I know also that that will not suffice. But if one went to them from the dead with a special message of warning, they will believe and repent.' What an illuminating message for the times in which we live is contained in the solemn response, 'If they do not hear Moses and the prophets, neither will they be persuaded though one rise from the dead'.

It is not more light that is the world's most pressing need, but more willingness to welcome the light which is already shining, and more readiness to walk in the path which it illuminates. We Christians know that One has risen from the dead. The bodily Resurrection of Jesus Christ is the crowning fact of history. But the unshakable evidence of that sublime event does not suffice to dissipate the patent indifference or the practical infidelity that is so widespread among even professedly Christian people. No argument will convince those who do not wish to believe. 'The path of the just is like the shining sun, that shines ever brighter unto the perfect day' (Proverbs 4:18). But the divine illumination, however brilliant it be, shines in vain upon all who prefer to keep the blinds down, who take pains to shutter up the windows of the soul. 'This is the condemnation,' said the Master, 'that the light has come into the world, and men loved darkness rather than light, because their deeds were evil.'

# Chapter 6

# GOODNESS AND SEVERITY: IN THE JUDGEMENTS OF GOD

'Let not the wise man glory in his wisdom, let not the mighty man glory in his might, nor let the rich man glory in his riches; but let him who glories glory in this, that he understands and knows me, that I am the Lord, exercising lovingkindness, judgement, and righteousness in the earth. For in these I delight,' says the Lord (Jeremiah 9:23–24).

But God demonstrates his own love toward us, in that while we were still sinners, Christ died for us. Much more then, having now been justified by his blood, we shall be saved from wrath through him (Romans 5:8–9).

But there shall by no means enter it anything that defiles, or causes an abomination or a lie, but only those who are written in the Lamb's Book of Life (Revelation 21:27).

Blessed are those who do his commandments, that they may have the right to the tree of life, and may enter through the gates into the city. But outside are dogs and sorcerers and sexually immoral and murderers and idolaters, and whoever loves and practices a lie (Revelation 22:14–15).

I N this final chapter I shall endeavour to exhibit some of the cardinal truths and abiding principles which may be gathered from the study of the judgements of God, as they are revealed in the representative examples which we have contemplated in the preceding pages. I hope also to demonstrate that although God has from time to time intervened in so drastic a manner that the stamp of divine severity has been impressed upon the page of the Scriptural revelation, yet throughout it all the goodness of God can be clearly discerned.

It will be seen that I have devoted a considerable portion of space to the vindication of the historicity of the great events recorded. To treat these grave happenings in the past as baseless myths, or empty legends, is to play directly into the hands of the Satanic enemy of God and man. Ridicule is a weapon more powerful than argument for the destruction of faith and of loyalty to the divine Lord. How much frivolous talk to no good purpose has been expended, for example, upon the Genesis story of the Flood and Noah's ark of preservation! But, if what is written is proven indeed to be a record of indisputable fact, with a typical significance of momentous solemnity, as the testimony of Christ himself reveals, then there is no room for ridicule but much room for reflection.

The great enemy of religious truth is not science, but superficiality, and the blindness of those who do not wish to see. 'Seek and you will find!' It is a condition which is as searching as the promise is sure. To obtain the vision of divine truth one must tread reverently, not trample proudly the courts of the Temple of the Lord. No one should presume to criticise or condemn any statement in the Holy Scriptures until great care has been taken to become thoroughly acquainted with its precise content and context. The writings of Moses and Isaiah, of Luke and Paul, should be treated at least with the respect which is freely accorded to the writings of Milton and Shakespeare. For, apart from its divine inspiration, there is a profundity in Holy Writ which is certainly not surpassed by these two renowned masters in the realm of English literature.

In the survey of the examples of divine judgement which have been presented, there have arisen certain truths and principles of surpassing importance which need to be forcibly impressed upon the hearts and minds of the people, especially in this time of world-wide strife and struggle for the preservation of liberty and integrity in the earth. They may be conveniently summarised under the following heads: (i) The Sovereignty of God; (ii) Divine Judgements Continually in Operation; (iii) The Indispensability of the Biblical Revelation; (iv) The Consummation of the End of the Age; (v) The Last Judgement: The Crisis and the Cross.

## (I) THE SOVEREIGNTY OF GOD

Our pre-eminent need is to rediscover the Sovereignty of God, and to recognise him reverently as the Creator, the Ruler, and the Sustainer of all that is. We are in no degree self-contained. We live moment by moment, breath by breath, according as he wills. Our physical life pulsates by his permission. 'In him we live and move and have our being.' Therefore, all that we think and do, all that we plan and purpose, should be directly and consciously related to him.

In scientific circles it is increasingly recognised that God is supreme in the realm of nature. It is impossible to carry on research that will satisfy without the assumption—whatever the name—of the existence and operation of a living God as a First Cause. The universe cannot be explained, as some once fondly thought, on a materialistic or mechanistic basis. Clerk Maxwell, that most brilliant scientist of a former generation, used to say: 'I have looked into most philosophical systems, and have seen that none will work without a god.' Every fresh scientific discovery deepens in the minds of the thoughtful the sense of wonder at the architecture of the earth and of the worlds in space; and wonder is not far removed from worship.

No explanation of the origin of things can displace the majestic declaration with which the Bible opens: 'In the beginning God created the heaven and the earth.' Feeble but futile attempts have been made to disprove it. In the nineteenth century elaborate experiments were organised to demonstrate the spontaneous generation of life from dead matter. It marked a pitiable retrogression; Aristotle, we know, believed that fleas and frogs and eels could be developed out of lifeless mud. He laid down the law: 'Every dry body becoming moist, and every moist body becoming dry, engender animals.' He lived a long time ago! But in our own times the Darwinian doctrine of Evolution has been engineered to endeavour to demonstrate the same gigantic fallacy. Granted only a single protoplasm in the slime, and the whole ordered universe proceeds automatically, without any superior direction, from the protoplasm! What a monstrous idea it was! Yet it caught on. It became extremely popular. Why? Because it served the useful purpose for many, of getting rid of the consciousness of God. Everyone who is determined not to believe in a divine process of creation, is compelled to fall back upon a theory of spontaneous generation, and an evolution proceeding therefrom. The creed of many even today might be summed up in the doggerel of Erasmus Darwin, in his *Temple of Nature:*

> Hence without parents, by spontaneous birth,
> Rise the first specks of animated earth.

To this cause we can trace much of the irreligion that is so manifest in our midst. God has no place whatever in the minds of a multitude, because in their ignorance they fancy that science has disproved his existence.

But truth must ultimately prevail. Wishful thinking has to give way to reality. As far back indeed as 1864 it was scientifically established, by means of precise experiment by Pasteur and others, that spontaneous generation never occurs. Pasteur, lecturing at the Sorbonne, before a distinguished audience, said:

> I have taken my drop of water from the immensity of creation, and I have taken it full of the elements fitted for the development of inferior beings. And I wait, I watch, I question it, begging it to recommence for me the beautiful spectacle of the first creation. But it is dumb—dumb ever since these experiments were begun several years ago; it is dumb because I have kept it from the only thing which man cannot produce—from the germs which float in the air—from Life, for Life is a germ and a germ is Life. Never will the doctrine of spontaneous generation recover from the mortal blow of this simple experiment.

The materialism of the closing years of the nineteenth century has now practically disappeared as a philosophy, but its aftermath has deeply affected the moral and spiritual life of the community. The late Lord Balfour said: 'We know too much about matter now to become materialists.' But what is freely admitted in the realm of scholarship may be far removed from the thinking of the

masses of the people. False theories may be completely
exploded in the halls of science, but the pernicious results
of those theories are not easily dissipated. 'A lie may
travel half round the world before truth can get its boots
on to go in pursuit.'

Writing in 1930, Dr Ronald C Macfie, in his inspiring
volume, *Science Rediscovers God*, sums up the present
position by a telling comparison:

> In the present state of scientific knowledge, science, unless
> it postulates a God, ceases to be rational and scientific. In
> the last decades of last century, biologists believed that
> Darwin had solved the mystery of life, and that mind was
> merely a by-product or an end-product of chemical processes.
> ... But today—though of course there are exceptions—
> Modern Science, as a great scientist, Millikan, puts it, 'of
> the real sort, is slowly learning to walk humbly with its God,
> and in learning that lesson it is, even as physics has learned
> the mystery of matter, contributing something to religion'.

But it has to be emphasised that the godless aftermath
remains. Dr Macfie quotes Professor Dwight as saying in
1911:

> We have now the remarkable spectacle that just when many
> scientific men are of accord that there is no part of the
> Darwinian system that is of any great influence, and that
> as a whole the theory is not only unproven but impossible,
> the ignorant half-educated masses have acquired the idea
> that it is to be accepted as a fundamental fact.

> If that spectacle [adds Dr Macfie] were remarkable in 1911,
> it is even more so in 1930, and in 1930 it is still to be seen.[1]

We thus today face the alarming fact that, impelled by a
science falsely so-called, a science proved to be unscientific,
the thought of God—his existence and his sovereignty—
has been dismissed from the consciousness of a multitude

---

[1] pp. 258–259.

of people in our midst, the majority of whom have made at least a formal profession of membership of the Christian Church. The result is a problem which in some respects is more baffling than that which confronts the Christian missionary labouring in heathen lands. Around us is a generation growing up in an atmosphere of practical infidelity with total unconcern about the things of vital religion. It constitutes perhaps the biggest menace to the welfare of the nation and empire. No new order of any abiding merit can be attained until this pernicious plague of practical infidelity is eradicated.

Still more do we need to recover the idea of the sovereignty of God in the moral life of mankind. 'The starry firmament above and the moral law within' are foundation facts in the realm of our being which only a fool dare ignore. Conscience is the still small voice of our Creator speaking to us in the depths of the soul. God's commandments are not only written upon the page of Holy Scripture; they are inscribed also upon the receptive tablets of the heart. And he is not far from any one of us. Yea, 'nearer is he than breathing and closer than hands or feet'. We need to remind ourselves continually of those elementary principles of religion taught us in our childhood: God you see me! God you hear me! In God's book of remembrance all my thoughts, words and deeds are being recorded. '"Can anyone hide himself in secret places, so I shall not see him?" says the Lord; "Do I not fill heaven and earth?" says the Lord' (Jeremiah 23:24).

The seriousness of life is enhanced by the consideration that all unconsciously we may be broadcasting day by day from earth to the very Throne of God and the presence of the recording angels. Who can set a limit to the possibilities of wireless transmission? Every sound travels. Science now declares that every spoken word may possibly be perceptible in far distant places in the universe. In God's wonderful world there may be an immense cosmic transmitter and receiver, and one day—the great day of revealing, all our spoken words—praises or curses, blessings or blasphemies—may resound again to our justification or our condemnation. For we have it on Christ's authority that 'every idle word men may speak, they will give account of it in the day of judgement. For by your words you will be justified, and by your words you will be condemned' (Matthew 12:36,37).

Therefore, our duty towards God and the sense of our moral responsibility need to be inculcated with renewed emphasis. One has sometimes heard the querulous complaint of a section of modern youth: What has life to give me? Such an attitude is obviously false. The world, as Keats said, 'is not a vale of tears, it is a place of soul-making'. The great foundation purpose upon which human life is built and made splendidly worth while is summed up in the inspiring declaration of the Scottish Catechism: 'Man's chief end is to glorify God and to enjoy him for ever.' We are not here merely to have a good time; we are here to do our duty towards him who has endowed us with the breath of life and the powers of sight and reason, of faith and imagination; above all, with the capacity for fellowship with the divine. We begin to live only after we have begun to realise that life is a trust, an endowment, a vocation, and an apprenticeship. We have been created not for the pleasures of time, but for the pursuits of eternity.

A serious reflection follows. Because God is the sovereign Lord Omnipotent, he can not only create: he can also destroy. And here it should be remembered that in the eyes of the Almighty the death of the body is not the supreme calamity which it appears in the eyes of men. There are worse things than death. Many a broken-hearted father and mother, could they have foreseen the foul deterioration which they have actually witnessed in the career of a prodigal son or daughter, would have chosen rather that their offspring should die in infancy and innocency. The death of the body is a minor incident in comparison with the corruption of the soul. Dr Alexander Whyte suggests a bold speculation. He writes: 'Jeremy Taylor, who has given immense learning and intellect to all such cases, says that God sometimes accepts a temporal death in room of an eternal … while Augustine, I see, and some other great authorities, are bold to class the awful case of Ananias and Sapphira under that Scripture of the apostle where he assures us that some church members are delivered unto Satan for the destruction of the flesh, so that the spirit may be saved in the day of the Lord Jesus.'[1]

Whether there be any real ground for that speculation I am not concerned to enquire. What is abundantly clear, however, is that Christ taught his disciples that they need have no fear of merely human persecutors who can only kill the body; but that they should rather fear the Almighty God, who has power to sentence both the body and the soul to the destruction of Gehenna. 'And do not fear those who kill the body but cannot kill the soul,' he said; 'but rather fear him who is able to destroy both soul and body in hell' (Matthew 10:28). The wastage of human life in the devastation of the Deluge, or in the destruction

---

[1] *Bible Characters:* Vol. V, p. 193.

of the Cities of the Plain, may appear to some to be so appalling as to deserve condemnation; while in the sight of God it is only a necessary cleansing process leaving a blessing in its train. Why should a morally rotten life be prolonged—a life which is of no benefit to the one who lives it, or to the community of which it forms a part? Why should God permit to continue that which corrupts in the present, and at the same time hinders the fulfilment of his gracious purposes for the future? For God is not particularly concerned about the length of life in the mortal body: he is concerned about the quality of the life of the immortal soul. He looks down to see not so much what we are in time, but what we are becoming for eternity.

## (II) DIVINE JUDGEMENTS
## CONTINUALLY IN OPERATION

In the preceding chapters of this book I have presented five signal examples of the operation of divine judgement in the affairs of nations and individuals. What we are now concerned to remember is that the judgements of God are continually in operation, not least in our own day and generation. History has never been a placid stream of perpetual progress. There has been growth and decay, advance and retreat, improvement and retrogression; for a fight of opposing forces has never ceased to be waged. Earth has been a cosmic battlefield, an area of unceasing conflict. 'I will put enmity between you and the woman, and between your seed and her seed; he shall bruise your head, and you shall bruise his heel.' This early prophecy in Genesis is seen in process of fulfilment in the history of the ages.

The struggle of the nations in the terrestrial sphere is, in the opinion of many, the reflection of a fierce conflict ever proceeding in a celestial sphere—between good and evil, right and wrong, God and the devil—between angels of light and demons of darkness. The fight for truth and purity by the Christian Church is figured in the language of Paul in weighty terms: 'For we do not wrestle against flesh and blood, but against principalities, against powers, against the rulers of the darkness of this age, against spiritual hosts of wickedness in the heavenly places' (Ephesians 6:12). Ultimately war is waged for the triumph or defeat of righteousness in human relationships. Because of that fact we discover that Israel, though a divinely chosen race, is severely punished for her national iniquity, and a mighty militarist nation like Assyria, though pagan, is the instrument of her chastisement. At other times she is miraculously protected and preserved. Throughout, the omnipotent and over-ruling hand of the Lord God of Hosts is revealed. When Jerusalem was besieged, after some forty cities and towns had been captured by Sennacherib, the Assyrian king, and he could proudly boast, as recorded on one of his clay cylinders now in the British Museum that he had shut up Hezekiah 'like a bird in a cage', the finger of God was seen in a mysterious pestilence that walked in darkness, which in a single night destroyed 185,000 soldiers in the Assyrian army. Jerusalem was preserved, and the prophecy of its divine protection, vouchsafed through Isaiah to Hezekiah, was fulfilled. What a dramatic intervention was that which is described in the prophetic words of Jehovah spoken to the proud Assyrian king: 'Because your rage against me and your tumult have come up to my ears, therefore I will put my hook in your nose and my bridle in your lips, and I will

turn you back by the way which you came' (2 Kings 19:28).
And all this happened as the result of a divine response
to sustained prayer on the part of a king and his subjects.

Deliverances, such as even non-Christian writers have
not hesitated to describe as the Miracle of Dunkirk, and
the Battle of the Marne, may reasonably be ascribed to
the intervention of some divine power, like the protection
of Jerusalem in 1917, when, so some affirm, was witnessed
a literal fulfilment of the prophecy of Isaiah: 'Like birds
flying about, so will the Lord of hosts defend Jerusalem.
Defending, he will also deliver it; passing over, he will
preserve it' (Isaiah 31:5).

Babylon was the proud mistress city of the world in the
days of Nebuchadnezzar. Yet its downfall was divinely
determined and predicted. In my collection of archæological
lantern slides I have one which is of peculiar interest. It
was made from a negative lent to me by a friend who
photographed the scene himself, while residing in
Mesopotamia. It is a desert place. No habitation, no
building of any kind, is in sight. In the background a line
of railway can be faintly discerned. In the foreground
are two Arabs—an elderly man and a younger woman.
Over their heads there is a printed notice in English and
Arabic which just says 'Babylon—Halt'. That is all that
remains of the great and glorious metropolis of the world,
so proudly presumptuous in the days of Nebuchadnezzar,
and of his successor Belshazzar, who was slain at its capture
in the midst of an impious feast. And here is the inspired
prophecy of its downfall uttered some twenty-five centuries
ago: 'And Babylon, the glory of kingdoms, the beauty of
the Chaldeans' pride, will be as when God overthrew
Sodom and Gomorrah. It will never be inhabited, nor
will it be settled from generation to generation; nor will

the Arabian pitch tents there, nor will the shepherds make their sheepfolds there. But wild beasts of the desert will lie there, and their houses will be full of owls; ostriches will dwell there, and wild goats will caper there. The hyenas will howl in their citadels, and jackals in their pleasant palaces. Her time is near to come, and her days will not be prolonged' (Isaiah 13:19–22).

With that ancient prophecy compare this modern story. Dr Cyrus Hamlin, a distinguished missionary, tells us that when he was in Constantinople some years after the Crimean war, a colonel in the Turkish army called upon him, and in the course of conversation which ensued, demanded some proof that the Bible is the Word of God. The missionary replied by asking him the question: 'Were you ever in Babylon?' The Turkish colonel immediately replied: 'Yes, and I had a most curious experience. I am very fond of sport, and I had heard that the ruins of Babylon abound in game; so I determined to go there for a week's shooting. Knowing that it was not safe for a man to be in that desolate region except in the company of others, I engaged a sheik to accompany me with his Arabs. We reached Babylon and pitched our tents. A little before sunset I took my gun and strolled out to have a look round. The holes and caverns in the mounds which cover the ruins are infested with game, which, however, are rarely seen except at night. I caught sight of one or two in the distance, and then turned my steps backwards to the encampment, intending to begin my sport as soon as the sun had set. Imagine my surprise to find the men striking their tents! I went to the sheik and strongly protested, as I had engaged him for a week. Nothing I could say, however, would induce him to remain. "It is not safe," he said. "No mortal flesh dare stay here after sunset. In the dark, ghosts, goblins, ghouls, and all sorts of things come out of those caverns, and whoever is found here is taken off by them and becomes one of themselves." I offered, if he would stay, to pay him double the price agreed upon. "No," he replied, "I could not stay here for all the money in the world. No Arab has ever seen the sun go down on Babylon. But I want to do what is right by you. So we will go off to a place about an hour distant and come back at day-break." And go off they did.'

The judgements of God are continually operating not only in the rise and fall of nations and empires, but also in the lives of men and women individually. A distinguished physician has said, 'Nature never forgives and never forgets'. There is a law operating without cessation in our bodily constitution, and judgement proceeds according as we obey or disobey. The dipsomaniac, the drug addict, the inveterate sensualist, soon begin to manifest the operation of the law that the wages of sin is disease and premature decay. What is true in the realm of the body is equally true in the sphere of the soul. There is a moral order in the world, however dimly it be discerned. No man can continue to do wrong with impunity. There is a judgement ceaselessly dogging his footsteps as he proceeds on his evil way. Napoleon was by nature a king among men. But he fell. Emerson sums up his character in the words: 'He did all that lay in him to live and thrive without moral principle. It was the nature of things, the eternal law of man and of the world, which baulked and ruined him; and the result, in a million experiments, will be the same.'

These words might indeed be regarded as prophetic of the fate which awaits a modern dictator of lesser breed than the Corsican. He has dared to flout the moral laws, written and unwritten, upon which the whole universe is established; but, though the clouds be dark overhead, we can yet discern the overruling Providence of the righteous government of a sovereign Lord Omnipotent. A day will surely dawn which will witness a catastrophic collapse like to that of the downfall of Babylon, when again the question will be asked: 'Is this the man who made the earth tremble, who shook kingdoms, who made the world as a wilderness and destroyed its cities, who did not open the house of his prisoners?' (Isaiah 14:16–17). 'The mills of God grind slowly, but they grind exceeding small'—in the lives of nations and of individuals; for the judgements of God are continually in operation in the earth and in the habitations of mankind.

## (III) THE INDISPENSABILITY OF THE BIBLICAL REVELATION

If I were asked the question: What is our premier need as the condition of a new and better order in the future? I should immediately answer: To put the Bible back into the hands of the people and to bring the hearts of the people back to the Bible, to read and respect it as God's Word to man—his Guide of Life for time into eternity. We recall the impressive verdict of John Richard Green, the historian, concerning the condition of our land at one of the most formative periods of its history: 'No greater moral change ever passed over a nation than passed over England during the years which parted the middle of the reign of Elizabeth from the making of the Long Parliament. England became the people of a book, and that book was the Bible ... everywhere its words, as

they fell on ears which custom had not deadened, kindled
a startling enthusiasm. … The whole temper of the nation
felt the change. A new conception of life and of man
superseded the whole. A new moral and religious impulse
spread through every class.'[1]

The indispensability of the Bible is as manifest as is its
sublimity. No other literature can be compared with it
for the illumination which it provides concerning the
most pressing problems of human existence. What am
I? Whence came I? Whither do I go? For a solution of
these fundamental questions, which arise spontaneously
in the minds of all thinking men, whither shall we go?
Where science is dumb and philosophy is dark the Scriptures
are both eloquent and luminous. How amazing it is to
realise that the Bible has anticipated by thousands of
years some of the most recent discoveries of modern
science. The first chapter of Genesis carries upon its
surface the unmistakable evidence of its divine inspiration.
WE Gladstone, scholar and statesman, described it as
'this wonderful, this unparalleled relation, this inestimable
treasure'. What a convincing testimony is that from the
pen of a scientist of the first rank, Sir J William Dawson:
'We have here a consistent scheme of the development
of the solar system, and especially of the earth, agreeing
in the main with the results of modern astronomy and
geology. It would not be easy even now to construct a
statement of the development of the world in popular
terms so concise and so accurate.'[2]

Note the first creative fiat: 'Then God said, "Let there
be light".' No competent scientist of today would repeat
the sneering question of Voltaire: 'And how did the light

---

[1] *A Short History of the English People*, pp. 460–462.
[2] *Eden Lost and Won*, p. 50.

come before the sun was created?' The mystery of the nature of light is perhaps deeper today than at any time during the past century. Two opposite theories—the corpuscular and the undulatory—are held simultaneously. It is a rash proceeding to assume that the primeval light of the first day was sunlight. Of what nature it was precisely, the divine Author alone knows. But of the necessary priority of light in the scheme of the origin of things all scientists are now agreed. Professor Jeans has strikingly said: 'The whole work of creation might be summed up in six words: "God said, let there be light."' Thus the first creative word in Genesis, and the last decisive word in astronomical science, completely harmonise.

Note again in the first chapter of Genesis, how the Bible has corrected beforehand the rash conclusion of the thorough-going evolutionist that the manifold forms of life have evolved from lowest beginnings by gradual development, so that one species has been transmuted into another, overleaping the boundaries which separate them. Darwin, it is well known, confessed that he did not know of a single instance of such transmutation. And Professor Julian Huxley, in a broadcast utterance, recently affirmed that evolution had ceased except in the realm of mankind! In the light of all this recent discovery how marvellously accurate is the simple but profound Genesis statement: 'Then God said, "Let the earth bring forth grass, the herb that yields seed, and the fruit tree that yields fruit according to its kind, whose seed is in itself, on the earth"; and it was so. ... Then God said, "Let the earth bring forth the living creature according to its kind: cattle and creeping thing and beast of the earth, each according to its kind"; and it was so' (Genesis 1:11,24).

Nature, we now know, has erected fences. Cultural improvements may be made inside the fence; but trespass is forbidden. Reproduction proceeds 'after its kind'; evolution presupposes a reproduction after another kind. Unfortunately for the evolutionist it does not happen.

But it is especially concerning the purpose of human existence, and the ultimate consummation to which we are tending, that science is both dark and dumb. The Bible alone sheds a brilliant light upon the road. It shows us the goal of the race, and the way to its attainment. We are not creatures of a day; though the average span of human life upon the earth is less than forty years. We are created for immortality. God has put eternity in man's heart. 'Trailing clouds of glory do we come from God who is our home.' The duties and responsibilities of life, its pleasures and its pains, should therefore be viewed from the standpoint of belief that we are here only for a brief term of apprenticeship for a richer and more satisfying life hereafter.

I submit, then, that as one condition of a better order in the near future, a rich acquaintance with the Holy Scriptures should be inculcated as the foundation of all real knowledge, for every boy and girl born in the British Empire. TH Huxley, though himself an avowed agnostic, was compelled to pay tribute to the unparalleled influence of the Bible in the training of the young for the highest welfare of the State: 'The Bible has been the Magna Carta of the poor and of the oppressed. ... For three centuries this Book has been woven into the life of all that is best and noblest in English history. ... By the study of what other book could children be so much humanised, and made to feel that each figure in that vast historical procession fills, like themselves, but a momentary space between two eternities, and earns the blessings or the curses of all time, according to its efforts to do good and hate evil?'[1]

Germany exhibits today a glaring example of the pernicious results of rejection of the light which proceeds from the Word of God. For considerably more than half a century Germany has been the central source of that destructive Biblical criticism which is associated particularly with the name of Julius Wellhausen; who was a Professor in the University of Göttingen. Built upon a foundation of pre-suppositions of an evolutionary character, it has reared a superstructure of unbelief in the historic records of the Bible which is not far removed from incipient infidelity. But today its theories have been rudely shaken and seriously undermined by the historic facts of scientific archæology, so that its former adherents have begun to break away. Dr Albright, Director of the American School of Oriental Research in Jerusalem, has said that 'practically all of the Old Testament scholars of standing in Europe and America held these or similar (critical) views until very recently. Now, however, the situation is changing with the greatest rapidity, since the theory of Wellhausen will not bear the test of archæological examination.'[2]

It must not be forgotten, however, that this destructive criticism, which is now being discredited, has prepared the way in Germany for the creation of a new religion by the Führer and his associates. Alfred Rosenberg, the notorious prophet of this new Nazi type of religion, in his book, *The Myths of the Twentieth Century*, contemptuously rejects the authority of the Bible. In its place he substitutes

---

[1]  Orr, *The Bible Under Trial*, pp. 212–213.

[2]  *The Archæology of Palestine and the Bible.* 1932.

the 'German Soul'. Instead of the Gospel of Jesus Christ and him crucified, he proclaims a gospel of Blood and Race—the deification of the German nation which has become incarnate in Hitler, whose word is authoritative and final. It is a religion of racial bombast—a belief in the power of the blatant arrogance and intolerance of Teutonic supermen to be the masters of the destiny of nations in the future. One turns with relief to the statement of a German Pastor of the Confessional Church, who has recently written: 'If I may venture to say anything about the future of Germany, I can say only one thing—any reconstruction without the Biblical foundation will be useless. ... But I do believe that in the Confessional Church the beginning of a new order has emerged, an order in which God comes first, and his Word is believed and applied, no matter what the cost may be.'[1]

I submit that we in Britain ought to take warning when we remember what has occurred in the land upon which the light of the Reformation first shone. I repeat that our premier need today is to recognise the absolute indispensability of the Biblical revelation to guide us in our plans for a new order in the future. A revival based upon the Bible devoutly studied would work wonders in the moral conduct and spiritual aspirations of the community. Let the Word of God be widely read; let it make its own impression upon the minds and hearts of the young; let the growing generation get rich in the knowledge of the oracles of God. Upon that foundation we can with confidence build a nation and empire characterised both by moral purity and material stability,

---

[1] *World Dominion*, July, 1942, p. 211.

of which it might be said: 'God is in the midst of her, she shall not be moved'.

## (iv) THE CONSUMMATION OF THE END OF THE AGE

The necessity of the Biblical revelation for our own times becomes particularly urgent, when we reflect that it alone provides the basis for an optimistic outlook into the future.

Most non-Christian thinkers and writers today are candidly pessimistic. They are faced with frustration on a gigantic scale, and they can see no sign of amelioration in the future. Dreams of the inevitability of human progress have vanished. The grim facts of a brutal and bestial war, unparalleled in its magnitude and intensity, have given them a rough shaking and stirred up a rude awakening. Humanism is bankrupt. Lacking the consciousness of a living God who is ruling overhead, many are tempted to believe that our modern civilisation is destined to perish rather than to recover.

But the Christian believer, building his philosophy upon the Biblical revelation, can sing a song of praise even in the darkest night, especially when he sees, as he now does see, things coming to pass upon the earth which were divinely predicted thousands of years ago, as the Scriptures plainly testify.

Principal Cairns has opportunely emphasised the optimism which characterised the Christian Faith in its pristine purity. He says: 'I believe that we entirely miss the meaning of early Christianity if we miss the fact that it is an optimism, that, as Edward Caird once said, "Jesus

Christ was the greatest optimist that ever lived".'[1] The secret of this optimism is to be found in the consciousness which was so widespread in the early Church that though sin, and the misery which sin occasions, was everywhere present, and the tragedy of the Cross for the Christians as for the Christ could never be far away, yet beyond was the promise of a new and blissful order to be inaugurated by the personal return of their Saviour and Master Jesus Christ in power and great majesty. The Kingdom of God, they believed, would visibly and gloriously appear when the King should return.

The prophetic Scriptures of the Old Testament prefigure the Coming of Christ under two very contrasted aspects. A picture of humiliation and pain is presented on one hand, and a picture of honour and power on the other. In one the Messiah is described as a 'man of sorrows and acquainted with grief'; in the other he is shown as an All-conquering King and a Prince of Peace. Here was an apparent contradiction. It was a subject of wondering enquiry to the seers and prophets of ancient days. Peter describes the Old Testament prophets as searching diligently, investigating the time which the Spirit of Christ which was in them did indicate 'when he testified beforehand the sufferings of Christ and the glories that would follow' (1 Peter 1:10–11).

As we look out upon a distant mountain range, concentrating our vision upon two gigantic peaks apparently close together, which we discover later to be separated by a long valley lying between, so the Hebrew prophets could discern in the dim distance the coming of a Messianic Sufferer and the coming of a Messianic King; but they

---

[1]  *The Riddle of the World*, p. 250.

were not aware of the fact that a long valley of conflict and humiliation lay between. The early Christians, however, could distinguish between the Cradle, the Cross, and the Crown; between the first coming for Crucifixion, and the second coming for Coronation and the establishment on the earth of the Kingdom of God. It was when he, as apparently only a despised Nazarene carpenter, was being condemned to death by his ecclesiastical judges in Jerusalem, and charged by them to say explicitly whether or no he was the Son of God, that Jesus said: 'Hereafter you will see the Son of Man sitting at the right hand of the Power, and coming on the clouds of heaven' (Matthew 26:64). Concerning this unparalleled declaration, Luthardt truly says:

> Even the mad pride of Roman emperors who demanded religious homage for their statues has never gone so far as to conceive such an unheard-of thought, and here it is the lowliest among men who speaks. The word must be truth; for there is here no mean term between truth and madness.

This apocalyptic hope has been too long obscured in present-day Christianity. One manifest result is that the Church, for the most part, has worked according to a misleading plan and programme. We have tried to establish the Kingdom by our own efforts in the absence of the King. We have faded and pessimism abounds. Principal Cairns has rightly condemned the pessimistic versions of Christianity which are so widely current. 'These,' he says, 'are not confined to those parts of continental Europe which have suffered most in the war, where we might have expected them, but we find them in our own country as well. Dean Inge, for instance, holds that we have no ground for thinking that the course of history is leading on to some universal blessed consummation. How is this pessimistic view of history derived from the New Testament? It is got, I think, by the simple excision of the whole Advent element from the teaching of our Lord. ... It is clear that our Lord predicted his own return in glory and power, and that the great majority, if not the whole, of the early Church had that expectation. The New Testament outlook is certainly, therefore, upon the victory of God's Kingdom in the world of space and time, as well as upon the vaster background of eternity.'[1]

In that vision so dramatically presented in the last book of the Bible which begins with the procession of the Four Horsemen of the Apocalypse, we have exhibited what might be called a panorama of the characteristic events of the present age—the dispensation which lies between the two mountain peaks of the first and second coming of our Lord. 'And I looked, and behold, a white horse. He who sat on it had a bow; and a crown was given to him, and he went out conquering and to conquer.' The White horse is the symbol of Christ's conquests in the world through the preaching of the Gospel. It is a revelation of world-wide evangelism. But there follows a Red horse, and to him that sat thereon power was given 'to take peace from the earth, and that people should kill one another; and there was given to him a great sword'. That is a clear symbol of war. Next comes a Black horse, ridden by one who had a pair of balances in his hand, featuring famine, and the consequent rationing of food in the time of war. The fourth is a Pale horse, the symbol of pestilence— a symbol of widespread disease, like the plague of influenza which, beginning in 1918, caused a greater loss of life than resulted from the whole devastation of actual warfare in the four years and more preceding.

---

[1] *Op. cit.*, p. 251–252.

But the vision does not end there. Two more seals remain. In close conjunction there is pictured the noble army of martyrs—'the souls of those who had been slain for the word of God and for the testimony which they held'—and their poignant cry ascending heavenwards: 'How long, O Lord, holy and true, until you judge and avenge our blood on those who dwell on the earth?' The vision of martyrdom is followed by the breaking of the sixth seal, which introduces a twofold scene of terrestrial and celestial convulsion. Above, the sun and the moon are darkened, and the stars of heaven are falling—imagery of the collapse of kings and princes and human systems of government; while terrifying earthquakes occur below, symbolical of the confusion and distress and consequent anarchy and abject fear spreading, as is described, among all classes of men upon the face of the whole earth.

It is a sombre, solemnising picture; yet it is not the end, but it is immediately preparatory thereto. For after the sixth seal has been opened the way is prepared for the opening of the seventh, to be signalised by the personal return of Jesus Christ, who came at first as a Suffering Saviour to redeem, but who comes the second time as a Conquering King to reign.

White horse and red horse! The colours are strangely mixed. Gospel peace and blood of battle! What a remarkable conjunction! Who among men would have dared to prefigure it? Yet is it not true? Charles Wesley wrote, two centuries ago: 'O for a thousand tongues to sing my dear Redeemer's praise'. He little thought then that a day was not far distant when, as a result of world-wide evangelisation, the praises of Christ would be sung in more than one thousand languages and dialects of mankind upon the earth.

Evangelism and war! These are two outstanding characteristics of the present age which were foreseen by the divine Son of Man. And 'the testimony of Jesus is the spirit of prophecy'. In Matthew 24, which is commonly called the Prophecy on the Mount, we find that he plainly outlined the course of events which would intervene before his promised personal return. Not peace, but a sword, did he predict; not harmony, but division and apostasy; not unhindered spread of the Gospel, but opposition and excommunication, persecution, and martyrdom; and finally, notwithstanding all the resisting forces, he said: 'this gospel of the kingdom will be preached in all the world as a witness to all the nations, and then the end will come' (Matthew 24:14). And what a glorious end it will be—an end which marks the new beginning of a perfect order of peace and just government for mankind—an end which will be signalised by the armies of heaven accompanying the now triumphant Christ on his way to establish the Throne of God in the midst of the earth; for it is written: 'He has on his robe and on his thigh a name written, King of Kings and Lord of Lords' (Revelation 19:16). In a very real manner, but one which obviously is beyond the power of any exegete to describe, Jesus Christ is apparently destined to be crowned not far from the very spot which witnessed his humiliation and agony on the Cross of Calvary. He has taught us to pray, 'Your kingdom come'! And at last we are learning that the coming of the Kingdom is not to be effected by a gradual reformation of man's making, but by the crisis of a divine intervention.

Thus with the lamp of inspired prophecy to illumine our path we may dare to behold the waste and want of war without absolute dismay. Notwithstanding the wickedness of masses of mankind, God is working out his purposes of blessedness for his redeemed. Evil may appear often to be triumphant, and we may be tempted to take up the martyrs' cry: 'How long, O Lord, how long?' But the very extremity of the world's suffering may be regarded by the faithful as a sign that 'the coming of the Lord is at hand'.

> Careless seems the great Avenger;
>     history's pages but record
> One death-grapple in the darkness
>     'twixt false systems and the Word;
> Truth for ever on the scaffold,
>     wrong for ever on the throne.
> Yet that scaffold sways the future,
>     and behind the dim unknown
> Standeth God within the shadow,
>     keeping watch above his own.

The Second Advent is a great glorious theme, with various aspects which cannot be completely illustrated in a work such as this, that has its own limited objective. But at the risk of digression, let me say that I do not believe that we are, in this age, merely working up to a final collapse or crack of doom. On the contrary, I believe that the Almighty God is working gradually but very surely according to a definite all-embracing plan; and, as part of that plan, the true Church, which is the mystical Body of Christ, is even now being educated and trained and disciplined so as to have an honoured and responsible position of administration in the new divine order that is to be. I believe in the reality of the Saints' Reign so clearly predicted in both the Old Testament and the New Testament Apocalypse; and correspondingly, a translation of the saints as a necessary preliminary to that majestic royal return of our divine Lord for which we consciously or unconsciously pray when we say, 'your Kingdom come'. This, I urge, should be the Church's supreme objective— the one blessed hope of all who build upon the promises of God; who watch with loins girded and lamps burning, eagerly expectant for that glorious Messianic Appearing which prophets have predicted and about which angels have sung; for that golden millennium of peace on earth and goodwill among men, when just administration shall operate and wars shall cease, cannot be until he who came at the first in the manger to suffer and to die, comes again in the clouds of heaven to conquer and to reign. 'For unto us a child is born, unto us a Son is given; and the government will be upon his shoulder. And his name will be called Wonderful, Counselor, Mighty God, Everlasting Father, Prince of Peace. Of the increase of his government and peace there will be no end' (Isaiah 9:6–7).

## (v) THE LAST JUDGEMENT: THE CRISIS AND THE CROSS

A supreme crisis in the history of the individual soul is reached when, illumined by the light of the Gospel of the grace of God, the searching question is faced: What must I do to have a part in the great transformation that is divinely destined? What must I do to be eternally saved? The question becomes increasingly serious in the light of the fact, so patent on the pages of the New Testament, that the saved represent only a portion of mankind. They are described as the 'few who are chosen'; they are called 'a people for God's own possession'—selected out of all the evangelised nations of the earth. The Church is not essentially an ecclesiastical organisation; it is essentially a selected and separated company of men and women who have individually responded to the summons of the Gospel, and have surrendered themselves to the service of Jesus Christ, whom they acknowledge as their Saviour and their King. Said the Master: 'I know my sheep, and am known by my own.' These are now being educated, trained, and disciplined, under the superintendence of the Holy Ghost, for co-operative service with God and his Christ in the future regeneration, which is to be both here upon the earth and in some other of the many mansions of the Father's house.

The crisis of decision for the individual soul becomes one of transcendent importance when it is realised that the Cross of Christ is a great divider. The tragedy of Calvary points to three fundamental realities. It reveals the punishment which of necessity falls upon sin and transgression of God's holy laws. 'The soul who sins shall die'; for 'the wages of sin is death'. Secondly, it reveals the divine provision of a way of escape. 'Behold! The Lamb of God who takes away the sin of the world!' A highway has been set up by which banished ones may return; the Cross has broken down the barrier by which all who have been alienated from God through sin may be restored to fellowship with the Eternal. 'God was in Christ reconciling the world to himself'; for 'Christ also suffered once for sins, the just for the unjust, that he might bring us to God'. But the Cross on Calvary proves also in the experience of men to be a sharp divider. Before it no neutrality is possible.

On the first Good Friday there was exhibited to the whole world what might without irreverence be described as a dramatic illustration of the divisive power of the Cross of Jesus. Two gangsters, as we would call them, were suffering

the drawn-out agony of crucifixion by the side of Jesus—
one on his right hand and the other on his left. Those two
malefactors were marvellously alike—partners in the
committal of crime, in the confession of their guilt, in the
condemnation which they justly deserved; they were also
partners in the sacred company of Jesus during the hours
of their crucifixion; and, at the beginning, they were
partners in reviling the silent Sufferer at their side. But
before the end there was a change. One of the two became
solemnised and impressed. He had never before seen a
man suffer so silently as this Nazarene by his side. Presently,
as death approaches, the eyes of his soul are opened; he
has a vision which reveals at once his need, and the power
of this Jesus, who claims to be the Christ, to meet that
need. 'Lord, remember me when you come into your
kingdom.' The penitent cry pierces the heart of the silent,
suffering Saviour. Immediately comes the response:
'Assuredly, I say to you, today you will be with me in Paradise.'
What a bounty was thereby bestowed! 'Today—what
promptitude! With me—what company! In Paradise—what
bliss!' It has been truly said that of the two thieves who
met at the place called Calvary, one was saved that none
may despair, and only one that none may presume.

But a separation took place there and then which is
symbolical of what is proceeding universally wheresoever
the Gospel is preached. And the gulf is widening. Sometimes
the question is asked: Is the world growing better or
worse? The true answer appears to be both better and
worse. The light tends to become brighter and the darkness
more intense. Dr Reinhold Niebuhr has recently said: 'It
is significant that the New Testament invariably pictures
human history as moving towards a climax in which evil
becomes more naked and unashamed, pride more arrogant,

and conflict more overt.'[1] In his last letter to Timothy, Paul draws a dark prophetic picture of the corruption and apostasy which will characterise the end of this age: 'But know this, that in the last days perilous times will come: for men will be lovers of themselves, lovers of money, boasters, proud, blasphemers, disobedient to parents, unthankful, unholy, unloving, unforgiving, slanderers, without self-control, brutal, despisers of good, traitors, headstrong, haughty, lovers of pleasure rather than lovers of God, having a form of godliness but denying its power. And from such people turn away!' (2 Timothy 3:1–5).

Thus the Cross creates two humanities which are being sundered more and more, as time proceeds. One of these two humanities is linked up with Christ in preparing for that new age which is so clearly destined and demanded. In God's programme for the new order, a threefold process has been revealed—the regeneration of the soul, the resurrection of the body, the renovation of the heavens and the earth. Here, those who are in Christ experience in their own persons the first great transformation which is part of the divine plan. 'Unless one is born again, he cannot see the kingdom of God.' This, according to Jesus, is the prime necessity. The self-surrender of faith in Christ brings into operation immediately the regenerating power of the Holy Spirit; so that 'if anyone is in Christ, he is a new creation'. But, on the other hand, rejection of Christ and his transforming power, by those who have heard the proclamation of the Gospel, entails a hardening process within the heart. The last state of such is worse than the first.

---

[1] *Europe's Catastrophe and the Christian Faith,* p. 35.

This sharp division in the world of mankind, especially that portion of it which has been evangelised, is becoming accentuated as the age proceeds to its final consummation. Then the gap already existing will be immeasurably widened, and a gulf fixed which shall never be bridged. For there is a great divine event impending to which the whole creation moves. It is described in the oldest creed in Christendom in the words: 'He shall come to judge the living and the dead.' No more solemnising truth than this can enter into the inmost soul than that the Christ, who came at the first to be a self-sacrificing Saviour, is coming again to be our judge. Paul, preaching to the Athenians on the Areopagus, presented his Gospel with grave urgency when he said that '[God] commands all men everywhere to repent, because he has appointed a day on which he will judge the world in righteousness by the man whom he has ordained. He has given assurance of this to all by raising him from the dead' (Acts 17:30–31).

Who shall stand when he appears? Who can with calmness and confidence anticipate that great day of Christ's Apocalypse? Only they who have in real penitence knelt at the foot of the Cross, beholding with awe yet with gratitude the wounds of the crucified Redeemer; who by faith have received from his pierced hands the free gift of pardon and peace, and the power for newness of life— all procured for us by the atoning death of him who 'bore our sins in his own body on the tree'. For 'he was wounded for our transgressions, he was bruised for our iniquities; the chastisement for our peace was upon him, and by his stripes we are healed' (Isaiah 53:5).

The Cross continues to be a great divider. It stands at the parting of the ways. In his day Paul testified: 'For the message of the cross is foolishness to those who are perishing, but to us who are being saved it is the power of God' (1 Corinthians 1:18).

It is no different today. However we may explain it, experience teaches that human nature left to itself tends to deteriorate and become corrupt. There is a law of gravitation in the moral sphere which, unless counteracted, drags men down to things earthly, sensual, devilish. But the Cross reveals that the mighty hand of God is outstretched from heaven to earth—reaching down to save and uplift the perishing souls of sin-diseased men and women. Some grasp the Mighty Hand and are held; others refuse it, or ignore it, or despise it. And thereby a division is created in the realm of mankind.

Our eternal future rests upon decision—especially upon the decision which concerns our present personal attitude to Jesus Christ, the world's Redeemer. For ultimately his words are decisive: 'He who is not with me is against me.' And the issue is momentous. The soul of man lies between two fires. On the one hand is the fire of the purifying grace of the Holy Spirit, which is out-poured upon every true believer in Christ; on the other is the fire of a divine judgement, which is destined to purge away all the dross and refuse of human kind, in an everlasting destruction from the presence of him whose eyes cannot for ever behold iniquity.

The judgements of God in the past have been lesser judgements—anticipations and indications of, the Last Judgement—the final separation, so simply, so solemnly, yet so unmistakably portrayed in the testimony of our Lord and his apostles. It requires no profundity of scholarship to assess the awful significance of these prophetic words which proceeded directly from the lips of the Master himself: 'When the Son of Man comes in his glory, and all the holy angels with him, then he will sit on the throne of his glory. All the nations will be gathered before him, and he will separate them one from another, as a shepherd divides his sheep from the goats. And he will set the sheep on his right hand, but the goats on the left. Then the King will say to those on his right hand, "Come, you blessed of my Father, inherit the kingdom prepared for you from the foundation of the world": ... Then he will also say to those on the left hand, "Depart from me, you cursed, into the everlasting fire prepared for the devil and his angels": ... And these will go away into everlasting punishment, but the righteous into eternal life'. (Matthew 25:31–46).

# ALSO PUBLISHED BY
# QUINTA PRESS

**Jonah: Patriot and Prophet by DE Hart-Davies**

A simple explanation of the meaning of the book of Jonah.

**Visible Saints: The Congregational Way 1640–1660 by Geoffrey F Nuttall**

A new edition of this classic work on the development of Congregationalism in the 17th century.

**Studies in English Dissent by Geoffrey F Nuttall**

A collection of essays and articles written by Dr Nuttall between 1943 and 1977.

**Manual of Congregational Principles by RW Dale**

The definitive work on the principles of Congregational church government.

**Christian Fellowship or the Church Member's Guide by John Angell James**

A simple manual on how church members should relate to each other, to their minister and to other churches.

### The Anxious Inquirer by John Angell James

The very influential evangelistic book of the Victorian age.

### The Works of George Whitefield on CD-ROM

Includes facsimile and reset versions of Whitefield's Works and hymn book, a reset version of his Journals and several biographies. It is hoped that a fuller, printed, version of Whitefield's Works, including many previously unreprinted sermons and unpublished letters, and a new edition of the Journals based on the original editions, will be made available in the future.

### Greek to the Rescue by Terence Peter Crosby

An introduction to the value of New Testament Greek for those who have not learnt (and probably don't want to learn) the language.

### On Eagle's Wings by Hazel Stapleton

A book of practical advice for those suffering from ME. Written from a Christian persepctive.

### The Standard Bearer by David Rayner

A biography of the Christian educationalist and campaigner for public morals, Charles Oxley.

### The Family Portrait by David Gray

An examination of the Bible's practical teaching of family life.

# IN PREPARATION

### History of Congregationalism by RW Dale

Completed after his death by his son, AWW Dale. Covers the period from the time of the Apostles to the end of the nineteenth century, concentrating on the period from the Reformation.

### A Defence of Congregational Principles

A collection of the writings of John Cotton on church government (including *The Keys of the Kingdom of Heaven* and *The Way of Congregational Churches Cleared*), with Thomas Hooker's *Survey of the Summe of Church Discipline,* the Apologetical Narration, the Savoy Declaration of Faith and Order, and The Cambridge Platform.

### The Autobiography of John Angell James

The autobiography with editorial comments by his successor, RW Dale, and his son, Thomas James.

### The Works of John Angell James

Based on the 16 volume edition edited by his son after his death.

### The Collected Writings of PT Forsyth

We hope to publish all the books, articles and letters of this influential Congregational theologian.

### The Life and Sermons of Christmas Evans

Paxton Hood's biography printed with Evans published English sermons.

### The Welsh Religious Revival 1904–05
### by J Vyrnwy Morgan

A critical evaluation of the Revival and especially of Evan Roberts. Quoted by all subsequent histories.

### The Welsh Religious Revival

A collection of contemporary newspaper accounts published by the *Western Mail* as a series of booklets.

### The Romance of Primitive Methodism
### by Joseph Ritson

A brief history of the denomination, founded in the early 19th century, that decided that Methodism had become weak and flabby.